Carolyn,
May your angels and your men :) continue to surround you!

♡ Rachel

start IT UP

A phenomenal true story
of eternal life & love

RACHEL PEARSON

Start It Up: A Phenomenal True Story of Eternal Life & Love

Cover Design by Fresh Design
Feather and green texture ©Shutterstock and Fresh Design

Interior Layout & Typesetting by Melissa Williams Design

Edited by Julie Klein and Kira Poncin

ISBN: 978-1-7339324-1-7 (paperback)
ISBN: 978-1-7339324-0-0 (eBook)
ISBN: 978-1-7339324-2-4 (hardcover)
First Edition

www.rachelpearson.net

Introduction

The term *God* may represent judgment or exclusivity to some, and *heaven* may sound like a place far away. *Spirit* may elicit fear or suspicion within a person, and the term *died,* or *death,* may sting. I use terms in this book that come most easily and feel good to me. For me, *God* represents divine love, connection, and the source from which all love, healing, and creation comes.

I do not use the term *heaven* in reference to a geographical location but to a spiritual state, as I believe heaven lives among us. The *other side* is a shortened phrase I use for the other side of the veil, heaven. I interchange the terms *spirit* and *heaven* and *the other side* throughout this book. I also use *Spirit* in reference to connection made within the holy spirit. I refer to *death* only in the physical sense.

Terminology is necessary for human expression, but any term I use is a label and, as such, will be limiting and inadequate to describe the infinite, boundless love that comes from God, Source, our Creator.

Prologue

It was July and it had been particularly hot and humid. I had gone to bed feeling grateful for A/C and cool sheets at the close of a long, muggy day. I found myself startled upright in bed from a deep sleep. Through the blinds of our master bedroom patio doors, I saw flashing lights atop a car. I do not know if the lights woke me up, or if I woke up and then saw the lights. My husband, Craig, was still sleeping.

I squinted and saw two male uniformed police officers approaching our home. One walked slightly behind the other. It was a rare occasion when anyone unintentionally arrived at our door because we lived on a hill in the middle of five acres. As I tried to assess the situation, memories began to flash before me from eight years ago, when we built our home.

We had found the perfect property for us. On the edge of our small city, we would be close to amenities and the land was only "gently sloped" according to northeast Tennessee standards. Craig carved out just enough woods, building our home into the property, rather than taking away from the land's natural landscape.

The first item purchased for our build was a tractor. All the kids enjoyed driving and working the tractor from the safety of Dad's lap. At that time Perry was eight; Rayanna, six; Jonas, three. Perry and Rayanna could help haul wood, but they mostly explored and made up their own games. We spent countless Saturdays as a family on our new property.

We were all so excited when we could finally move in. Our south-facing great room had large windows that provided gorgeous blue views of the mountains in winter; a green, tree-filled landscape in summer; a glorious painted-by-nature scene in autumn.

The bottom of the property was grassy and level; this was where our driveway began and where we planted apple and pear trees (that never did bear much fruit) and blueberry bushes. Going up the drive and to the left, hidden in the woods and brush, was a precarious treehouse Perry built, equipped with a clay oven he also built. Directly across on the right side was a treehouse later constructed, with more expense and integrity, by Craig and all three kids. I wanted to crawl into memories when I saw the officers approaching our door, walking on our brick walkway.

I didn't want to process what was happening. My mind wanted to focus on the walkway. I could see patches of moss attached to the bricks and green growth popping up between the holes in the bricks. I wanted to be anywhere but in the present moment. I wanted to escape into the past.

The brick walkway was a family project we completed about two years after we moved into our home. Perry had run back and forth between playing in his fort and handing bricks to me. Perry had built this fort, his first one, with help from Granny, my mom. He built it next to our house, alongside his dad.

Perry made his own game out of helping with the walkway, rushing to see what he could accomplish with whatever project he had going on at his fort before I'd call on him again.

Rayanna had patiently and cheerfully remained close by my side to help lay the bricks, while she also tried to get Jonas involved. Jonas was so happy to oblige Rayanna. He had to use both of his still-dimpled little hands to give bricks to "Sissy."

That single memory brought to mind only a few of the special qualities I loved, and still love, about each of my children. Perry could be difficult to motivate, but he would put his own twist on what he would otherwise consider boring chores or activities. I'm sure he is still putting his own twist on things.

Rayanna delighted in learning, especially when it came to new projects. She enjoyed encouraging her little brother to do more than he, and sometimes we, thought he was capable of. It would not be untrue to say Rayanna is still Jonas's strongest motivator, and she is still a voracious learner. She is currently a focused, full-time college student and part-time research assistant.

Jonas was a happy-go-lucky child who seemed to love anything, as long as one of us was with him. Being in our company was what Jonas enjoyed the most. Jonas agreeably tried new things if it involved helping others or being with others whom he liked. Jonas still enjoys our company, and he will gladly offer a hand to help someone out, even if it involves a project or activity he doesn't care for.

The harsh, bright beam from the officer's flashlight stunned me into the present moment. It was a Friday night. Perry was sixteen and he'd recently obtained his driver's license, so he was the only one of our kids who could have been away from home that night. Yet I knew he was home.

Earlier in the evening I had interrupted a Skype conversation Perry was having with his friends. I said goodnight to him, told him not to stay up too late, reminded him to turn his phone in and told him I loved him. I loved that he still mumbled, "Love you, too."

The kids' rooms were on the second floor and the master bedroom was on the main floor of our home. The computer was in the dining room, also on the main floor, where Perry had been Skyping with his friends. I heard Perry chatting as I got into bed.

I couldn't recall hearing Perry go to bed before I fell asleep, but the internet shut off on a timer and Perry had a routine of going to bed when it shut off. Surely he was upstairs sleeping. He had to be home.

The kids always dropped off their electronic devices on a table in our bedroom as they went to bed. At this point, Perry was our only child who had a cell phone. I looked to see if Perry's phone was on our bedroom table, but it was too dark.

I had given goodnight hugs to Rayanna and Jonas. Did I see them go to bed? More questions and thoughts swirled around in my mind, causing my heart to race and making it difficult for me to focus.

I found myself at the front door, looking down at the threshold separating me from whatever it was I didn't want to know. I didn't want to open the door. I wanted a permanent barrier. I wanted time to stand still. And I didn't understand how Craig was still sleeping!

Panic began to intrude my entire being. I was sick to my stomach and suffocating at the same time. I watched my hand open the door. I saw a shiny glimpse of silver. A badge. *I don't need to see your badge!* I had already lived an eternity-filled minute with awareness of the police officers' presence.

My head felt like it was going to explode from confusion when I noticed one of the officer's lips moving. I was unable to hear his words, yet I knew what he was saying.

There had been an accident. Perry.

I heard an unfamiliar, deafening noise and I was unable

to process that its origin was from my own body. Then Craig was holding me, and we were in bed. It had all been a nightmare.

I released a flood of violent tears that carried away the residual terror. Craig checked on Perry and reported back he was sleeping soundly. All our kids were sleeping. I thanked God and eventually settled back into the peace that comes from knowing all my babies were safe and sound, under our roof.

1

High Waters

My disturbing dream occurred in 2014. Peace returned that night, but I would never forget the experience. I can't remember if it was before the dream or after, but around this time a strong desire to clear our physical surroundings and downsize our belongings hit me. Happy that the kids were all mature enough to sort with little guidance from me, I enlisted (and probably bribed) my family to help.

Organization has never been my strong suit, so I surprised myself with my new passion, and I even enjoyed this summer project. Later, through the lens of grief, I would experience regret that clearing clutter from our home had been a big focus that summer. It was short-lived regret because I would also see how this served to soften our fall, even if in the smallest of ways.

Fall 2014 through spring 2015 would turn out to be the most difficult season our family had experienced up to that point. It seemed we faced one challenge only for another one to arrive. Craig went into work at the start of 2015, right after Christmas break, to be told his position had been cut. It turned out that management possessed knowledge of an imminent corporate merger, and from a spirit of fear, acted to ensure management's job security.

While I had held several different part-time and temporary jobs since Jonas had been a preschooler, Craig had been (and is) the primary income earner. His news was life changing for us. I was working part-time as a fitness, Zumba, and line dance instructor. I loved my work more than I had ever loved any work outside the home, and I loved that I could work ideal hours around our family's schedule. I added classes to earn extra money, but my income alone could not support our family.

Craig's abrupt job loss occurred not too long after a person in authority projected shame on Perry over a simple, forgetful, and innocent mistake he had made at school. A spirit of fear was behind this situation as well; reputation took highest priority, and excessively so. If the same occurrence had involved a peer of Perry's who had been more charismatic, more popular, or whose parents had been in high standing in our community, there most likely would have been no incident at all.

This season turned out to be trying, in one way or another, for each member of our family. I began to feel as if the universe was beating up on us. It wouldn't be until early June that I would feel life's edges begin to soften.

Craig and I did a decent job of channeling our energy into his job search. Craig was (and is) an IT security professional. There were only a few jobs of his position in our region, none of which were open. Willing to take a pay cut, Craig applied to other IT jobs, but he got no bites. He gradually expanded his search outward until March, when he accepted a consulting position in Dayton, Ohio, six hours from our home. I stayed behind with the kids to finish out the school year while Craig traveled home most weekends.

There were too many variables preventing us from initially making long-term plans, the least of which were we would need time to process a permanent move and sell the home we had built. We made a tentative plan to rent for the summer and resolved to make more specific plans later.

Rayanna and Perry wanted to know that, if we moved, it would be a permanent move. They wanted definitive answers, as we all did. We didn't feel like we would be returning to Tennessee if we moved, but Craig and I wanted to at least wait until we moved—to know how we were all faring in Ohio—before speaking with certainty.

Rayanna experienced her own difficulty throughout spring, which she now recalls as her most personally challenging time. Things did seem to be going smoothly for Jonas, but maybe that was why he'd grieve the most over our upcoming move.

My heart hurt for each member of my family throughout this season. It surprised me that Perry and Rayanna, our older kids, were most open to the idea of a permanent move. Given the challenges they had experienced, it also made sense.

I began to wonder if a move could turn out to be a rainbow after our flood of unfortunate events. I wondered if maybe the move was supposed to happen, and every challenge served to help us loosen our attachment, our grip, onto what we had considered our permanent home and lifestyle.

Either way, I trusted that all things would work for the good, and I gripped tightly onto my faith that there was a higher plan being knitted together behind the scenes.

There were bright spots during this season of high waters. My cousin Nichole, who is like a sister to me and aunt to my kids, got married in the spring. I encouraged Perry to invite his friend Mahalia to Nichole's wedding. Perry loved Mahalia and she loved him, even though their relationship was a friendship.

Aside from getting ready for his first formal high school dance, the only time I can recall really seeing Perry nervous was around Mahalia before Nichole's wedding. Perry wanted my opinion on what to wear. After giving him my advice, I tried to stay out of his way and not embarrass him on that lovely evening I so fondly remember.

Close to a year after Perry passed, Mahalia shared with me the following:

"I can't explain to anyone how special I felt to be loved by him. I never could fully realize how amazing it is to love and be loved by someone until I lost him . . ."

Another fond memory from this time is Easter, our first nonconventional Easter. The kids and I traveled to Ohio for the weekend to spend Easter with Craig. Perry's friend Ronnie went along. Craig had been staying at an Extended Stay. We rented two adjoining rooms in a separate hotel, to house us all.

I remember so vividly all the joking and laughter from that weekend. I took the kids' Easter baskets with us, included one for Ronnie, and filled them in Ohio. We surprised the kids with Easter baskets on their hotel nightstands. There were mishaps in finding last-minute candy, messes with hot dogs, and adventures with melted chocolate, all of which added to the joyfulness of that light and happy weekend.

Traveling to Ohio that weekend, we had played the Beatles non-stop for the entire trip. I love the Beatles, so this hadn't bothered me. Perry sang loudly and off-key, as he often did in the car. Perry also liked to sing around the house, not so loudly. He had favorite songs he would sing or hum for weeks and sometimes months at a time.

From his last year with us, I remember Perry singing "Piano Man" by Billy Joel and "Hello, Goodbye" by the Beatles. He sang "Hello, Goodbye" so much, I wondered if he was ever going to stop singing that song. When planning his memorial, it came to me that "Hello, Goodbye" would be one of the songs to be played. The most perfect song.

The highlight of spring, notably for Perry, was his birthday party at our house in Tennessee. We had his party on his birthday, Friday, May 8. I encouraged him to invite all his friends. Family friends and family attended as well. Craig drove down from Ohio to make it home in time for Perry's party to start.

Perry's party turned out to be another nontraditional family event—the first of our kids' birthday parties for which I was incapacitated. I woke up to a stomach flu on his birthday.

Craig wouldn't be back until it was time for the party to start, so I worried about party prep. Perry came into my room after he got home from school that day, confused as to why I was lying in bed in the afternoon. He told me he was sorry I was sick, asked if he could get me anything, and eagerly offered to pick up the pizzas, snacks, and other grocery items.

Craig arrived home in time for the party and a friend of ours, Terry, helped with serving cake, cleanup, and other tasks. After Perry died, for Terry's birthday her coworkers ordered a cake for her work party. The bakery made a mistake and the cake read, "Happy Birthday Perry."

My desire to move grew stronger as spring drew to a close. I fantasized about just hitting the road and moving early, but I couldn't go against my practical nature. The school year was too close to completion.

I even began to lose my passion for my work, which I had loved. I knew I would miss the people I worked with, many of whom were dear friends.

My feelings ran deeper than missing my husband; I experienced an impatient anxiety, a feeling that we were supposed to be elsewhere.

Maybe I needed to feel these feelings to stay motivated throughout the transition. I felt uncomfortable sharing my feelings with my family and friends, who were sad from the thought of us moving. Knowing how much they would miss us (and how much I would miss them), I didn't want to come across as insensitive, so I felt alone in not fully expressing my feelings to anyone other than Craig and the kids.

During this period before we moved, I had become suspicious of Perry's activities with his friends, which caused me to feel overwhelmed in general with parenting (mostly) on my own. My intuition led me to limit Perry's connections with his friends, which I knew would not go over well with him. For the last few weeks of May, I allowed him to continue to socialize with his friends, but only at our house.

Perry didn't like this limitation, predictably and understandably so. He told me he wasn't going to talk to me again. He only kept his word for a few days, but this was new territory for us that broke my heart. Everything felt wrong and out of place.

Craig and I found a townhouse in Ohio to rent. We signed a six-month lease and scheduled our move for the end of May. Knowing we would have limited space, we planned to take only what we would need or want for the summer. The previous summer downsize had eliminated approximately one-third of our belongings, making the task so much easier than it otherwise would have been. Later, this would make sorting through Perry's belongings less challenging.

Our emotional stormy season in Tennessee included our extended family. My grandmother had fallen and broken her hip in April. My dad's mother, Mary, was Granny to me, but Nana to my kids. She endured an extended stay in the hospital, followed by inpatient admission to a rehab center. She had been otherwise healthy, so healthy that we used to joke she'd outlive us all. She was a Type 1 diabetic but had taken immaculate care of her health for as long as I knew her, consuming a nearly perfect diet. She had just gotten off her treadmill when she slipped in her hallway and broke her hip.

For Mother's Day 2015, we put together a meal and took it to Nana at the rehab center. Perry and I did the shopping. Perry picked up AriZona tea, which he insisted we needed to take. Our family joined my parents and grandfather at the picnic shelter. Perry wheeled Nana outside, and she expressed so much happiness about us all being together. She raved about the meal and what a pleasant day it was. This was the last family occasion we shared with her, and it was my last Mother's Day spent with Perry.

Nana made a point of telling me on this occasion, and on previous visits to see her in the rehab center, that we would be "just fine in Ohio." This was not something I would have expected my grandma to say, so it took me by surprise. Of all people, I would have expected her to express how much she would miss us, yet she was the person who I felt most comforted and encouraged by during this time.

Nana expressed feeling restless, frustrated, and eager to return home while in rehab. She developed pneumonia shortly after our Mother's Day picnic, which quickly led to complications. She was admitted to the hospital, and we were told that she could only be made comfortable.

The end of my grandma's life here on earth corresponded with the end of our lives in Tennessee. Literally the same day. Craig and Perry went on ahead to Ohio with the U-Haul after they stopped in the hospital to say goodbye to us and a final goodbye to my grandma. Rayanna and Jonas stayed behind with me.

We sang Nana's favorite hymns to her and tried to ensure her comfort that night. Nana passed away the next morning with her family by her side. A few days later, Craig and Perry traveled back for her memorial. Craig and Perry both served as pallbearers.

Perry first said no to serving as a pallbearer, in the same way Perry's best friend would at first say no, two months later, to the overwhelmingly painful idea of burying someone he loved. Perry changed his mind, as did his best friend.

Nana thought the world of Perry. When Perry had gotten his license, Nana was excited and the family relieved to have another driver to escort her on all-day shopping excursions. She bragged about what a commendable driver Perry was and how patiently he would wait for her.

Nana frequently complimented Perry for how polite and helpful he was to her and my grandfather. Months before her fall, Perry was at their house helping with yard work when my grandma almost fell in the garage. Perry caught her, breaking her fall, and he helped her back up.

Nana told this story to whomever would listen. She knew it would have been so much worse had Perry not been there to catch her fall.

I believe that in some way, Nana later helped break Perry's fall and welcomed him Home.

2

A Fresh Start

We headed to Ohio after my grandmother's memorial. Craig took a separate vehicle, leaving before me and the kids. When we left, Perry and I took turns driving. I was impressed by his road-trip, highway driving skills. We talked about Ohio and new opportunities we would have there. Perry rattled off names and facts about several Ohio state colleges. This was a pleasant surprise to me, and I found Perry's random and obscure trivia about each school to be fascinating.

Perry talked to me more on that trip than he had in weeks. The energy between us seemed to be clear and flowing, and I remember distinct moments of feeling tension dissolve that had existed between us a few weeks prior. The storms were behind us and the sun was out.

Our rough season had taught me that home is not a structure of permanence... Home is wherever we are together, whenever our hearts are open. We were on the road, yet home, and I could see the rainbow.

Perry and I played a music trivia game on our trip that we often played. He recited trivia or lines of music, and I guessed the artist or song. When I got it right, it was my turn. I always gave him '80s music because Perry knew music from the '60s and '70s better than he knew '80s music. I was the loser for years until I convinced Perry to change the rules to a multiple-choice format. Then it became more of a competition.

While we traveled, we discussed how Cincinnati would have cooler concert venues. Perry asked me if I would go to a Rolling Stones concert with him. I told him yes, I would.

As we neared Ohio that night, I drove and had Perry get out my U2 *Rattle and Hum* CD with the extended commentary. Somehow, Perry wasn't very familiar with U2. Over the years, I thought I had played for him all the '80s music I had ever owned. I had taken every opportunity to tell him stories about songs from the '80s. I still don't understand how it passed me by that I had never introduced Perry to U2! I joked about failing as a parent because he was only vaguely familiar with a couple of U2's songs, so we had to listen to the entire CD.

Perry seemed mesmerized by the music and Bono's commentary. Sharing this ordinary time with him felt extraordinary. I drove us toward the night-lit Cincinnati skyline listening to "I Still Haven't Found What I'm Looking For," "With or Without You," and Bono's talk about social justice and finding God in unlikely places. It was one of those magical and rare times together that, even as it was happening, I knew I would never forget.

We weren't listening to music Nana liked, but I wouldn't be surprised if she was with us that night. Or maybe the presence of our angels filled the air. Maybe both, and more. All I know is Spirit was very close to us. I felt such sweet relief, hope, and loving connection with my son.

Less than six months after that night, I was living in Arizona (with my family) when I attended a line dance event in Las Vegas. It was my first time dancing after believing I would never want to dance again. My heart was tender, but I met up with friends from back east who surrounded me with love and comfort, while also giving me ample space I needed so soon after Perry's passing.

At the dance event, my friend Cindy wanted to introduce me to a line dance instructor who lived near me in Arizona. Soon after our conversation, Cindy and I ended up in the same class. I stood next to Cindy as she spotted the instructor she wanted to introduce me to standing in the row in front of us.

The dance was taught to the same song, "With or Without You," instructed by Swedish choreographer Raymond Sarlemijn. I felt Perry with me in an intense way during the class. After the class, before I could tell Cindy I felt Perry with me, she shared with me that she felt Perry's presence with us in a powerful way.

Later that weekend in Las Vegas, I went to lunch with Cindy and friends. Over the speakers "Piano Man" by Billy Joel began to play. Cindy swayed and sang along in such a beautifully expressive way. I felt Spirit with me while Cindy sang, and I could hear Perry's voice singing along with Cindy and Billy Joel.

Unbeknownst to Cindy, Perry used to sing this song around the house. As I recall this memory now, I feel such gratitude for Cindy's brave and passionate spirit, for sharing such intimate connection with me and Perry.

3

Beautiful Goodbye

As if the death of a loved one isn't painful enough, many young people die in unexpected and sudden ways, leaving their loved ones in an agonizing absence of goodbye. This trauma can feel unbearably searing for a parent. As a mom, I have always felt a deep sense of meaning and responsibility in protecting my children, kissing their boo-boos, and easing their fears. When this mattered most to me, I felt denied my very purpose in life. I have felt no deeper sense of rejection.

It was the greatest insult upon the greatest injury to not hold my son as he took his final breath. Much time and emotional release would be required, but Spirit would help me shift my perspective to see the beautiful goodbye I had shared with Perry.

I took this picture of Perry at the amusement park Cedar Point in Ohio, a few weeks before his death.

Perry wanted to ride roller coasters years before he reached THIS TALL on the signs. Once Perry became THIS TALL, we celebrated his birthday two years in a row at Carowinds, the best amusement park near our home in Tennessee.

Immediately before I took the picture above, I hesitated before my typical, "Turn around and lemme take a picture." I decided to capture the view of Perry walking into the sunset. It's interesting to me now that most of the pictures I took of Perry in Ohio were taken from behind.

Sometimes not knowing is a gift. For as much as I would have wanted to know if it meant I could have prevented my son's death, how could I have enjoyed our time together if I had known Perry was going to die?

I only knew that my young man was growing and maturing as I blinked. I only knew that he would be leaving soon, and I wanted to appreciate every moment he was under our roof, still ours. The present moment was, and still is, all that ever matters.

Perry and I woke up early for the three-and-a-half-hour drive to Cedar Point, arriving when the park opened. We rode every roller coaster that day, many twice. As an adult, I'm not a roller coaster aficionada, but I developed a strategy to ride with our kids: I keep my eyes closed for much less of an adrenaline-fueled experience.

Perry was nothing if not observant, but I didn't think he noticed my eyes were closed during the first ride. We were secured in the second coaster when he smiled and said, "Mom, open your eyes this time!"

I did manage to avoid one ride. It wasn't a coaster, just a vertical ride with a sudden drop, and I knew my stomach would drop with it. I noticed the ride consisted of two units, with two separate lines. Perry and I got placed in alternating lines, so pretense became an extremely tempting option! I hemmed and hawed, but when I got to the entrance, I told the attendant I needed to leave.

When the ride ended, I beelined to the exit. I tried to fake excitement and breathlessness to the best of my ability so I wouldn't be in the awkward position of having to flat-out lie. I can't remember ever having done so to my kids, and I wasn't sure I could fake it well. Immediately after he got off, Perry asked, "Did you ride it?"

"Why do you think I didn't ride it?" I asked. Perry laughed. "Mohhm!" I began laughing and he teased me, exclaiming how he couldn't believe that his own mother would try to deceive him.

While walking around the park and chatting, I brought up house hunting and how he might like a basement bedroom. I knew he'd be leaving for college soon, but I had his senior year and future visits home in mind.

"Wouldn't a basement house be nice . . ."

Our words overlapped when Perry replied, "I'll be gone."

Logically, I knew Perry was referring to flying the parental coop, but his words penetrated my entire being. "I'll be gone" lingered, hanging in the air like an ominous word bubble.

I tried to shake it off. "But there will be holidays and summer break . . ."

"Mom, I'll always come home." Perry's reply was passionate and seemed to fit what I had felt, more than it fit what I had said. In hindsight, I believe our souls communicated that day, and this exchange was the difficult part of goodbye.

I remember the ride home that night so vividly, as if in technicolor. Perry did the driving. He cranked the volume up as we sang along to music on the radio. I made my best attempt at singing correct lyrics, and this amused him. With the windows down and sunroof open, we drove down straight two-lane roads, through miles and miles of farmland.

One can't drive too far in our familiar part of Tennessee without seeing houses dotted along the rural areas. This was Perry's first experience driving through a pitch-black night with nothing to see but fields for miles. I remember the stars being the only lights we saw for a long stretch. The road was flat and wide open, and it felt like our future was as well.

That wasn't the last time Perry and I shared laughter or connection, but that day was our beautiful goodbye. I just didn't know it at the time.

My parents and grandfather visited us for a few days in Ohio. Rayanna and Jonas went back with them to stay for a couple of weeks. Perry never asked to go back with them, and Craig and I enjoyed this time alone with Perry. It was during this time that we made our Cedar Point trip. Craig and I spent Father's Day alone with Perry, another atypical holiday.

I remember how it felt awkward to not have our younger two children home on Father's Day, but I was aware this could be Perry's last year at home, and I focused on how special this time was. We spent Father's Day cycling on a local rural bike trail. I logged a total of 23 miles while the guys rode over 50 miles.

Craig and I thoroughly enjoyed time with Perry over the course of two weeks, individually and together, as a family of three. We had meaningful conversations, and Perry shared with me things he hadn't previously shared with me, nor would have, in Tennessee, where he feared I would have shared the information with parents of his friends.

Craig and I were free from the responsibilities we had living on five acres with settled lives in Tennessee. We were away from all that had grown along with being rooted in one home, one town, one place for so long. While I wouldn't be able to see it this way for a very long time, Craig and I were gifted a very long goodbye with our son.

Many people I connect with now share of a remarkably poignant, loving, or joyful time spent together that may or may not have occurred immediately prior to the moment of their loved one's physical death. It can take much time, healing, and intention, but I believe it's possible we can eventually find rest in a peaceful goodbye… and maybe that's only possible when we can know without doubt there really is no goodbye.

4

Monday

On the morning of July 27, 2015, I knocked on Perry's door. I suspected I'd wake him up and he'd call out from his bed. Perry had a bowl of cherries in one hand and a glass of milk in the other when I said goodnight to him the night before. Craig and I heard Perry talking to his friends on the phone as we drifted off to sleep. I knew he was up much later than us, so I was surprised when he opened his door.

I asked Perry if he wanted to go to Meijer (a supercenter) with me later that morning or stay home and do his laundry. I had noticed he hadn't done his laundry over the weekend. "Laundry," he replied. Perry didn't like shopping and he was out of clean clothes, so I wasn't surprised by his answer.

Rayanna and Jonas went to Meijer with me to buy pool accessories. Meijer was only a few miles away, but it was our first trip to the store. On the way to the pool section, t-shirts I thought Perry might like caught my eye. Perry had grown so much—several inches over the couple of months we had been living in Ohio. The previous week I had taken Perry jean shopping. It was back-to-school season, so the timing was favorable for his crazy growth spurt.

Heading back home from Meijer, an impulse hit me to detour to the pet store and buy mealworms for Perry's female hedgehog, Stan. Perry had a thing for giving pets older male names. Bob, Sam, and Fred were a few of his favorites. Not only did he assign these names to our pets, but he nicknamed our extended family's pets, regardless of their given names or genders.

Stan was Perry's Christmas 2014 gift from me and Craig. He had wanted a pet hedgehog, so Stan was a welcomed and cherished gift. Perry had immediately wanted to buy mealworms for Stan, but the pet store was out of mealworms over Christmas break. I had told Perry we'd go back, but then Craig lost his job and Perry never asked again. Mealworms would be a winning surprise now, both for Stan and Perry.

We returned home. Perry half-smiled at the t-shirts with a simple "thank you." Perry was a terrible liar, so he used omission wisely. Omission and hiding became Perry's strengths to compensate for his weakness. Perry's half-smile told me the t-shirts wouldn't become his favorites, but he appreciated the gesture.

Perry wasn't ace at lying or fake smiling. He never did like to smile for a camera. When Perry was younger, he adopted a camera smile, but it wasn't his natural smile. He couldn't genuinely smile unless something gave him honest reason to grin.

I revealed the mealworms to Perry, and then a genuine smile spread across his narrow face. Perry headed up the stairs and I followed him into his room where he took a few mealworms out and put them in front of Stan. Nocturnal Stan wouldn't be coaxed out of her ball pose this time of day, not even for mealworms. It was an anticlimactic moment, yet it became a profound moment for me—the last moment Perry and I shared alone together.

Craig was uncertain about the length of his contract position, but we were satisfied with all the opportunities in the area for his type of work. We felt very secure in committing to stay in the area, at least until Perry finished high school, longer if we would want to.

Perry was ready to start and finish his final year of high school. He wanted to work, and I had helped him submit his first job applications—to Kroger and Burger King. He hadn't yet heard back from either place. The previous week, he looked up local Boy Scout troops on the computer. We had been encouraging Perry to complete his Eagle Scout rank ever since his troop dissolved his sophomore year of high school.

Perry had been a very active Scout from the time he was a Tiger Cub Scout in first grade, but he had never been motivated by earning awards. Perry enjoyed Scouting for the sake of Scouting, and to him the dissolution of his troop had meant he was done, too.

After Perry's memorial, a best friend of Perry's shared with me that Perry had completed more projects and had helped his friends in Scouting more than any other Scouts his friend had known. His friends told me how Perry always helped everyone else with their projects to help them earn their awards. They expressed to me how they felt Perry had accomplished more in Scouts than most Eagle Scouts accomplish.

This made me proud and grateful for all the Scouting memories Perry made. Perry was involved in a very active troop with outstanding leaders who modeled hard work and a high degree of integrity, with kindness. Craig shares many Scouting memories with Perry, and for this I am grateful as well.

Perry went for a bike ride in the afternoon. Walking, hiking, and riding his bike were activities I encouraged Perry to do, more so as time went on in Ohio. At this point, we were nearly eight weeks into our new venture. We all seemed to be moving past vacation mode and into settling-in mode.

Perry returned home from his bike ride on Monday afternoon after an hour, which was typical. He complained about the heat when he returned home. It was unusually hot and humid, but it was not typical of Perry to complain about the heat. Nor the cold, for that matter.

I advised Perry to drink extra water. He impatiently reassured me he was drinking enough. "I know, Mom." He got a glass of water, but it would later haunt me that I didn't see him drink it. Perry needed more prompting than his siblings when it came to matters of self-care and self-regulation. He often needed guidance the most, but he resisted guidance the most.

I was pleasantly surprised when Craig arrived home early from work that day. I had just begun dinner prep when I heard him conversing with Perry in the adjoining living room of our close quarters. Craig asked Perry if he wanted to go for a bike ride. Perry declined, saying it was too hot.

Recently, Craig and Perry had been biking several times a week after Craig returned home on weekday evenings. Perry had never turned down Craig's invitation to bike. Then Craig asked Perry if he wanted to go see a movie, but Perry replied there wasn't anything playing that he wanted to see. I wondered if Perry might be coming down with something.

Perry went outside to talk to friends on the phone while I was cooking dinner. He usually talked on the phone inside, but we had no privacy in our small townhouse, so I wasn't suspicious. At his age, I certainly would have wanted to talk to my friends out of my family's earshot, so I didn't inquire when he came back in through the kitchen. My concern that day was that he stay hydrated. I did have other concerns, but they were related to the next day.

Perry had been talking in the space between our townhouse and the neighboring townhouse. I could hear him on the phone through the exterior wall that separated us as I was making dinner. I couldn't discern his words, only that he made several quick phone calls. The nature of his conversations sounded more like what I would have expected to hear on Tuesday.

The brevity of the calls and the upbeat excitement and quickness of Perry's tone could have corresponded with giving directions and coordinating where to meet. Perry had grown increasingly excited for his friends from Tennessee to visit the following day, so this wasn't necessarily a red flag for me, but it did put me on alert.

A few of Perry's friends from Tennessee were due to arrive on Tuesday, the next day, for a visit. Perry had been excited about their visit ever since they had made plans several weeks prior.

Their plans had involved spending a day at Cedar Point. Perry had told me his friends wanted to get a hotel room near Cedar Point. His friends were all eighteen, while he was seventeen. We wouldn't allow Perry to spend the night away from home with just friends in a hotel room, but I told him I would be willing to caravan, allowing Rayanna and Jonas to visit the park, too. I would stay out of their way at the park, I told him, but he would have to return home with us.

A few days after that conversation, Perry told me the guys wanted to do some local hiking instead. We made sure Perry knew his friends were welcome to crash at our place, where he would have to stay, but he told us his friends preferred to get a hotel room.

After dinner on Monday evening Craig and I decided to go for a short walk by a nearby house that was for rent. We asked the kids if they wanted to go with us. When we asked Perry, he said he wanted to go for a bike ride. We told him that was fine, and he headed out the door.

That was all normal, if not a bit unexpected since Perry

had complained about the heat earlier and had declined his dad's offer to bike. But it was dusk, and the day had begun to cool off. I asked Perry if he was feeling better and he assured me that he was. We figured as we usually did, that biking was a good outlet for Perry's energy, especially with the excitement of his friends' visit in the air.

Craig and I followed Perry out the door. I reminded Perry to be careful, to come home before dark. He always had. People were coming and going in the parking lot, so I refrained from saying "Love you!" Perry took off in one direction before we turned to walk in the opposite direction. I lingered, admiring the image of this fast-growing young man, riding off into the sunset. I knew these days were numbered.

I couldn't recall Perry ever returning home from a bike ride more than an hour later, and he had always come home before dark when he biked in the evening. We had never experienced any nights in Ohio, nor in Tennessee, where Perry hadn't returned home by curfew, nor times he hadn't returned our calls or texts. When it became dark and Perry wasn't home, I got nervous. When he didn't return our calls or texts, I knew he was in danger.

We drove around the neighborhood in every direction. We came back home to check if Perry had returned. His computer was open to Skype, and from his account I asked his friends if they knew of his whereabouts. One of his friends (who hadn't planned to make the Tuesday trip) called me. He was the only friend of Perry's who responded to me that night. He knew Perry had gone for a bike ride, but that was all he knew. He reassured me he would contact Perry's other friends and pass the word along.

I wanted to go check the nearby water tower. On our first day living in Ohio, Perry and I had taken a walk around the neighborhood. As we approached a nearby park, we saw a water tower.

"Cool!" Perry said.

"Don't even think about it," I replied.

I knew his insatiable desire to conquer tall structures. Perry had a strong, innate affinity for climbing, ever since he had been a toddler. He crawled even after he walked because crawling could take him higher. He could climb like Spiderman and was just about as limber. At seventeen, he could still turn himself into a pretzel. Not only was Perry unafraid of heights, he seemed most at peace on a mountain peak, sleeping high in a hammock, or on top of his fort.

Craig and I split up to look for Perry that night. We walked and drove, taking turns in separate directions. With Craig driving, we decided to go to the trail we biked as a family on the weekends. En route, I saw an image of Perry in front of me, as if a projection from my mind's eye, lying facedown in grass. I knew he was unconscious, or worse. I also felt a strong pull away from the direction we were heading. I knew Perry was not in this direction and I told Craig to turn around.

We turned around and I urged Craig to stop and file a police report at the police station on our way home. I was paralyzed by fear and couldn't leave the car. I waited what felt like an eternity for Craig to return and say, "The police here can't help us because we don't live in their jurisdiction." It would turn out this was the correct police jurisdiction for where Perry's dead body would be found.

We drove to the police station we were referred to. It was eerily quiet inside. Two male officers helped us. They asked questions and I gave them a picture of Perry from my phone that I had just taken Saturday, *only two days ago*, while we were at an Irish festival in Dayton. I gave them another recent picture of Perry on his bike. I told them about the scar on his finger, from splitting wood over the winter.

"He has braces and contacts," I told them, "and he can't see without his contacts."

"He doesn't have his wallet." *He must be hungry.* "If he's injured, how would a hospital identify him?" I asked. No response to my question.

Perry had never been gone all night, not even past curfew! He had always called or texted. No, he wasn't homesick. Friends were coming the next day and he was excited, making plans. *Was. Why I am using past tense?*

Perry had recently made a female acquaintance in the neighborhood, we told the officers. He had walked with her a few times, in the evening. The police suggested he was with his new friend, or maybe he made another new friend. Surely he would be home in the morning. They'd file a missing youth report and patrol our townhouse complex. I knew this wouldn't help. We needed them to help us search.

I knew my son. Perry was intelligent, but the officers' replies didn't match what any young person of average intelligence would do. If Perry hadn't planned on returning home before dark, he most certainly would have waited until we went to sleep and snuck out, rather than walk out right in front of us. I knew he was in danger.

I left in frustrated panic that we weren't being heard, and I was angry at myself for always having to be so damned respectful with authority. Surely, I wasn't assertive enough, or they'd be driving around with us, helping us find our son. I wanted the police to listen to us as if their son or grandson had gone missing.

Craig and I felt helpless, yet we continued driving and walking around in the dark. We kept calling and texting Perry, and I kept checking his Skype to see if anyone had replied. Nothing.

We decided it would be wise to get a few hours of sleep and head out at daylight. Craig slept but I couldn't. I sat outside in a camping chair, checking my phone and calling the police station. "I'm sure he'll be home in the morning," was the last reply I received. I was sure that statement wasn't true.

This was the longest day of my life.

5

Hell

I woke Craig at dawn. We drove around, walked, and then headed home to get our bikes and hit the trail. We were driving back to the trail when I received a call from a detective that Perry's bicycle had been found. We were near the location we had been the night before—when I had the vision of Perry lying in the grass. Craig turned around and drove the couple miles to meet the detective.

We arrived at a grassy property just a short walking distance from our townhouse. I saw Perry's bike and I didn't understand why it was so close to the road. I wanted to vomit. I saw an old farmhouse facing us, clearly visible from the road. I recognized the house and property as we had driven by it many times. It had always seemed out of place, standing proudly, sandwiched between a gas station and more modern residential neighborhoods. I had always liked the farmhouse's testament to years gone by and possibly to owners who refused to let go of their property. I would never again think those thoughts about the farmhouse.

Craig parked on the shoulder of the road and we got out. We began walking on the driveway and I saw a creek to my right. I never knew there was a creek here. Water was moving swiftly. *Oh God, no.* An officer approached us and introduced himself. I didn't recognize him from the night before. Behind him, toward the back of the property, I saw yellow tape. My heart pounded in my throat.

I had never known how deep this property was, how far back it stretched. From the road, driving by, it appeared to be a standard residential lot, but it was probably an acre or more, with most of the land to the rear.

The officer asked us questions. Other officers moved around in the background, behind the yellow tape. I made myself speak, answering his questions. We gave additional information, anything we could think of that might help. "Go home and rest. We'll find your son," the officer told us.

Craig loaded Perry's bike on the bike rack. Without Perry. I called my parents in Tennessee. I told them what we knew. I told them they should come. We parked at our townhouse in silence, knowing we'd have to tell the kids Perry didn't come home last night.

We walked through our front door. Rayanna and Jonas were up. They greeted us with smiles. *Dear God.* Everything about this morning was getting harder by the minute. My world was collapsing upon me as I fought to keep my composure for the kids.

We waited in agony. Two hours passed. Our townhouse felt like a cave. I could no longer calmly wait. I kept thinking of Perry's bike near the road and I could no longer bear thoughts of him being picked up by someone. My mind fought off scenarios of him being dropped off and of the creek. *God, he's been gone thirteen hours, fourteen . . . God help him! PLEASE!*

I told Craig we needed to go to the police station for an update. He sprung up as if he, too, needed to move. We told the kids we'd be back shortly. Exiting through the front door, we stopped in place as we saw two police cars entering our parking lot. I squinted to see if Perry was in the back seat, but it was shadowed, too dark to tell.

The cars parked and two men got out. I willed them to

open a backseat door, letting Perry out. *Please!* But they walked toward us. I searched the dark back seats from where I was standing. *Maybe he's detained for questioning? Handcuffed? He's seventeen, does that happen? Can seventeen-year-olds get arrested? Maybe they need to question us first!*

One man was obviously a police officer, wearing the uniform. The other man was wearing a white short-sleeved button-down shirt. As he walked closer to us, I could see something embroidered on top of his breast pocket. The word CORONER came into focus.

Crying out, a sword of pain ripped through me, doubling me over. Craig caught me midway to the ground as I collapsed. A howl came from Craig and I didn't recognize his voice in it. The officer-detective asked, "Can we go inside?"

My babies are in there! Even in our apocalypse, I desperately needed to protect our children. I would have preferred for the whole world to witness the scene, except for our children. I couldn't form words. "Ne-no," I groaned, shaking my head back and forth. "Our kids."

The sun was shining. The previous evening, I was standing in this exact spot watching Perry ride off into the sunset. Craig and I walked. I brought up having Perry's graduation party outside on the lawn we would have. "Wouldn't it be nice to have it outside? We could rent tables . . ." The previous day I was standing here with mealworms for Stan and t-shirts for Perry.

Perry should have been hanging out with his brother and sister at the pool and filling out job applications. He should have been buying snacks for his friends who would be arriving soon. Craig and I should be laying down the ground rules. We should have been looking at house rentals, fantasizing over yards and basements.

HE SHOULD BE HOME!

My whole world, my life—present and future—erased.

Now here we were, in someone else's life. In no life at all. In hell. The coroner described how our son's body was found. Head injury. *NO.* Alone. Abrasions. *NO NO NO.* Minor. Peaceful. Autopsy. *NO NO NO NO NO!*

"Is there anything we can do?" the coroner asked.

YOU CAN'T BRING MY SON BACK!

Wait. "He would want his organs donated." I managed to sob out the words. Perry had informed me of his wishes less than two years before, while visiting a classmate's sister and her family at the hospital, after she had been in a car accident. She passed away from her injuries a year after her accident. Perry was holding flowers for the family while I was finding a parking space when he informed me of his wishes. His words made me cringe, especially given the circumstances, and I told him I would be outliving him. "I know, Mom, but if something like this happens . . ."

The coroner spoke about incompatible factors of heat and time. "I'm sorry," he said.

We turned to face our front door as Craig and I held each other. I turned to him, "We should tell the kids in our room." Both of us in some kind of surreal autopilot mode as we walked in, we told the kids we needed to talk in our room. I remember the longest walk up our short stairs. We gathered at the end of our bed where we huddled the kids as closely as we could, embracing Rayanna and Jonas, forming a circle.

I have no idea how long we all sat there wailing, crumpled over. When I could speak, and Craig could speak, we alternated telling the kids we would still be a family. Life wouldn't be the same, but it would be good again. We would be happy again. The words sounded rehearsed. *Who is speaking these words?* The words didn't come from us, but through us, and it wasn't just our children but all four of us who were being spoken to.

A few hours later, Craig and I would have to give my parents the news when they arrived.

6

Miracles

There are many grief-stricken moments I still remember in vivid detail from the first days, weeks, and months following Perry's death. Miracles also occurred, from the very first days, weeks, and months. What I realize now is that we experienced miracles because we had gone through hell. It's our heartbreak that caused heaven to intervene in tremendous ways.

After the news, Craig and I continued to embrace the kids until my parents arrived. At that point, we sent the kids outside, wanting to protect them from more trauma and pain. My parents had tried calling us, but we weren't going to give them the news while they were driving, so we put our phones away. They had called my brother Kevin to tell him Perry was missing. Of course, Kevin didn't know Perry was dead, so he texted Perry, asking him if he was okay. This was all unbeknownst to me and Craig, as we hadn't talked to my parents. Kevin received this text reply from Perry:

"I'm okay. I was just sleeping."

My brother shared the news of Perry's reply with my parents while they were on the road to Ohio. It had been an old number of Perry's that Kevin had texted, but it was a sign for us. I have no doubt this gave my parents enough peace to continue their trip safely, even though it would be difficult for them to hear the truth when they arrived at our place.

This was also a sign to give us comfort, to let us know that Perry didn't suffer. Everything was unknown at this point. All I could think about was Perry's bicycle propped up so closely to the road. I wanted to believe Perry's death was some sort of accident because I couldn't bear the thought of someone harming him. I couldn't process the idea that Perry may have gotten picked up by someone or may have been hurt. I wanted to know for certain that Perry didn't suffer, but there were no known witnesses.

My brother had sent his text to me as well, but I experienced a delay in receiving it. I hadn't checked my phone for the rest of the day after my parents arrived, so I am uncertain as to when I received it, but I saw Kevin's text in the middle of the night.

Craig and I were still awake in the middle of the night. We couldn't quit crying and hadn't slept. Our kids had fallen asleep with us and they were sleeping soundly. We didn't want to wake them up, so we went downstairs. My mom was either awake or she woke up when we came down. I asked her if she had any medication that could help us sleep.

It was ironic that we rarely took meds and had very little medication in the house, yet earlier that day the detective had to search our medicine cabinets and the rest of our home. The most painful part was that they took Perry's computer away. I understood this later; it's typical process for a mysterious death, but I hurt for my kids who had just received the news of their brother's death and had to witness the police searching our home, leaving with their brother's possessions.

My mom gave us Tylenol PM. Craig and I took it and

went outside to sit on the back patio. We sat in our camping chairs, facing the direction Perry took his last breath. We sobbed, holding each other. We sobbed into our laps, into our hands. I caught a brief respite and sat up, trying to breathe while I could, before the pain would again take over.

Craig had just sat up as well. Staring straight ahead in silence, in the center of my vision I saw a green shooting star land, straight ahead, in front of us. I looked at Craig and he looked at me. We looked at each other to validate that what we saw really existed. The star wasn't a figment of our imaginations, not a grief-induced hallucination.

Bright green sparks and long vapor trails lit up the sky. Green was Perry's favorite color. I had never seen a shooting star land and I had to ask Craig if it wasn't fireworks. It was as if the sky had put on a personal firework show, just for us.

Just a few weeks before, we had watched fireworks on the Fourth of July. I have a picture of Perry I took from behind. He is entertaining my cousin Nichole's little boys, and there is a large, bright green firework lighting up the sky.

Craig and I went inside to attempt sleep—the first sleep for me in nearly 48 hours. As I walked past the kitchen counter, a text flashing on my phone screen caught my eye. This was Kevin's text:

"Perry says he is okay. He was just sleeping."

7

God's Trail

My dad is a minister. He dedicated our babies to God. He baptized Perry and Rayanna. Most importantly, he adored Perry. How my dad found the strength to take charge and guide us through the days to come, when his own heart had been ripped out, was another miracle in our story. I can't count the number of memorials my dad has officiated that I myself have attended, but nothing could have prepared him for this. He sat me and Craig down and told us what to expect regarding all the decisions that would need to be made.

Time and mental processing escaped me in those early hours, days, weeks. I could only feel my anguish. My pain overwhelmed and exhausted me, to the point that I couldn't find capacity for conversation or ability for mental processing or planning. It would be months before I could sustain a regular conversation with anyone outside of my family or newly made bereaved friends. I coped by conversing via text and Facebook Messenger on my own time, and I just couldn't process any kind of small talk.

Much in life was a blur to me in the first few months of grief. The term *numb* doesn't resonate with me and my experience because I was anything but numb to my pain. My pain blurred out time and movement going on outside of my family. I lived in a bubble of anguish.

I could barely move, and I felt rushed through planning. I could barely function, let alone make decisions about my son's memorial service. I am so grateful Craig and my dad were able to take the lead and handle details. I'll never forget how our friends and family members helped us through it all, in practical and comforting ways.

A minister friend came to mind who I wanted to officiate, and a scripture came to mind I wanted to have read at Perry's service:

"Since his days are determined,
The number of his months is with You;
You have appointed his limits, so that he cannot pass.
Look away from him that he may rest,
Till like a hired man he finishes his day.
For there is hope for a tree,
If it is cut down, that it will sprout again,
And that its tender shoots will not cease."

Job 14:5-7

We drove Perry's body to Tennessee for the memorial service. Technically speaking, it was a Celebration of Life service, but I had never felt less like celebrating. A *celebration* of my son's life that had been instantly snatched from him, from us, when he had the whole world ahead of him . . . ? This felt cruel and misleading. I longed for denial but couldn't fake it. I couldn't bring myself to speak the words "celebration of life."

We traveled back to Tennessee for Perry's memorial and burial. My mom and dad transported Perry's body within a cardboard box, in their minivan. Craig, the kids, and I followed them in our Jeep. Perry's physical form, his potential, his hopes and dreams, our hopes and dreams for him . . . All were now dormant, contained in an oversized shoe box.

For several hours of our road trip, my parents followed a vehicle with a rear, oversized decal that read "God's Trail." We even stopped for gas and ended up behind this vehicle again. I was confused by God's steady presence during this agony that God could have prevented. Yet God sent us a divine procession that rendered our brokenness holy. A cardboard box was my manger.

Craig and I chose not to view Perry's body. We offered our kids the choice and didn't want to influence them with our decision. This is a situation that offers no do-overs, yet we left the decision up to them. We most likely would have viewed Perry's body with our kids, had they chosen to, but they didn't want to and admittedly, we were relieved.

I served as a hospital corpsman in the Navy many years ago. My specialty, which I did not choose, was histopathology. An aspect of my training and work was to assist with autopsies and manage the morgue. I was all too aware of effects that heat and time have on a human body's appearance after death, regardless of age or health.

Four years later, not viewing the body is a decision that none of us have come to regret, nor did it put us in denial. I am aware that viewing the body is often the right choice for many others. I just believe external opinions should stay out of personal decisions, so that those mourning can clearly discern how he or she needs to be led, for their highest good and healing.

I easily held onto the vision of Perry from when I last saw him looking perfectly healthy and whole, on his young-adult edge of grasping life. Perry had been a constant, front and center force in our lives for seventeen years; I didn't need to see his body to know he had died.

I would feel the emptiness of no reply when we said goodnight to him. I saw all the empty space his physical form had once filled and so freely moved in and out of. I felt the void where his presence had once been as a constant in my daily life. I heard deafening silence where there was once daily conversation. I felt my arms ache for his bear hug.

I would see Perry's untouched food in the fridge, his unopened contact lenses, the toothpaste that didn't need replenishing, the popcorn popper that ceased to be used, unopened college advertisements, the graduation announcements I wouldn't be buying, the dried-out mealworms, and shirts that never got worn.

I couldn't be in denial of Perry's death when I was overwhelmed with the absence of my son who I loved more than life itself.

I experienced additional grief related to Perry's memorial. I didn't get a lock of Perry's hair, nor his thumbprint, and nobody asked me if I wanted these things. I later regretted having parted with his shoes. Others viewed our son's body who hadn't seen Perry alive and well months or even years before they saw his lifeless shell in a private viewing we offered. Craig and Perry's siblings were pained by other things that took place during this time. We were all in so much pain.

Maybe our society can do a better job at providing space to mourn in our own way. There should be no set time or place or one-size-fits-all defined way of memorializing our loved ones. We shouldn't feel rushed for the sake of tradition.

A couple years ago, I met a bereaved mother who told me she laid her son's body out in her home, opening her home for loved ones to come by. Her only plans were to keep her son's body until she felt she no longer needed to. I had never heard of such a memorial in our modern age, but this really touched me. I felt her son loved it, as she honored what felt right for her. I'm not sure why we have to hurry through things, but I would love to hear more of personalized memorials in the future.

All in all, I experienced so much love during this time. The comfort, the love from others, is what I recall now when I think of the early days. People surrounded us with loving presence and everything we could have needed. Everything and everyone showed up at the perfect time. I was overwhelmed by grief, but I was also overwhelmed by love.

8

Be Brave

I didn't want to wear a black dress to Perry's memorial. I wanted to wear a light-colored dress with green vines or leaves on it. I didn't own any dresses like this, and I knew I wouldn't be shopping. This wasn't a style at the time, so I doubted anyone could even find a dress like this for me, but it's what came to mind as we were traveling from Ohio to Tennessee.

My cousin Angela showed up in Tennessee, from Chicago, with dresses she brought from her closet. I saw the dress I wanted, white with a green vine pattern, and it fit me perfectly. Rayanna picked out another dress of Angela's. It was green with large colorful blooms, and the dress fit her as well.

Our community showed up when we had no capacity to deal. My cousins, like sisters to me, stayed by my bedside at my mom's house. They made plans on my behalf and took care of me. My cousin Nichole went with my dad, Craig, Rayanna, and me to select a casket and make other decisions for the service.

Nichole became my foundation when I lost my own, collapsing over Perry's shoes I had to leave with the funeral home. Nichole was brave in her love for me, in so many ways

I will never forget. She was my roots, keeping me planted on the ground. Speaking of roots... Since Perry's death, Nichole has planted trees in Perry's honor, multiple times a year. I can't describe what a gift this is to my heart.

My mom has always been the most tireless hostess I know, but never had I seen her rise to the occasion like I did after Perry died. Her home became base camp. She kept going and greeting that week, even when her own heart was breaking over Perry and for me, for us. Yet she kept going, welcoming everyone.

My cousin Jennifer stayed by my side like my personal grief assistant from the moment she arrived in Tennessee for Perry's memorial. She carried my burden with me, taking on my pain as her own. She cried with me and listened to me express all my painful thoughts and fears. Jennifer never seemed afraid of what I had to say. She was my safe space to share whatever was on my heart, whenever I needed to. Jennifer gave me herself, and there is no greater gift she could have given me.

Other friends and family showed up and helped us in more ways than I can even remember, including our family from Montana. My sister-in-law Pam helped with cleaning and managing the food around my mom's house. Pam, with Rayanna, Nichole, and Angela, bought me new pajamas after Perry's memorial. At that point, the pajamas I had been wearing probably needed a decent wash, and I was grateful. For the week they were with us in Tennessee, my in-laws provided a much-needed sense of groundedness for our entire family.

My aunt Debbie took Jonas shopping and helped shop for other miscellaneous items we needed. Family and friends engaged our kids in games and conversation. An earth angel, Connie, kept food coming and ensured that there was plenty for all the guests that came and went. Our friends, along with Perry's friends and family, showered us with love and support.

After the memorial, Perry's friends shared funny stories, many of which we had not heard nor would have heard, I'm sure, if Perry was here in body. I've heard other bereaved parents share similar sentiments. This is an odd gift of sorts, but a gift to be certain. I learned what took place on one mysterious night a few months before Perry's passing, while we were living in Tennessee.

Perry had asked if he could go to his friend's house to hang out with his two best friends. Together these guys were like the Three Musketeers. It was a weekend, so we gave him permission, but after Perry left something didn't feel right to me. I asked Craig to call our friend, Perry's friend's dad, to confirm the boys' plans.

As it turned out, Perry's friend had told his dad he was coming to our house. I called Perry to find out where he really was. Perry tried to talk his way out of it, telling me their plans fell apart and he'd soon be home. I knew Perry knew he'd been busted.

Apparently, the guys met up at the nearby university campus, just a couple miles from our house. All the boys attended the high school on campus, so this was a familiar location. They thought it would be fun to climb the inside of the campus athletic center, a large dome-shaped building. It did not surprise me to hear this was Perry's idea, and of course he was completely sober. Perry had a strong affinity for conquering tall structures, and his need to climb had been my biggest worry for probably fifteen years.

The guys shared how nervous they were, and how calm Perry was. Perry's friends told me I had called Perry when they were at the height of the structure, and Perry stopped to answer my call. Yikes, that was probably a good thing I didn't know! We had always wondered what their plans really were that night!

I heard another story about how Perry and his friends

climbed a downtown building after school to hang out on the roof. I'm pretty sure this happened more than once. The best story may be one Jonas wanted to share.

Shortly before we moved to Ohio, one evening Perry woke Jonas up to ask him if he wanted to sneak out and go to G2K, a local video game store. They picked up Perry's friend on the way. That's all they did, and they arrived home safely, their parents none the wiser.

Other stories I heard were of a different nature. Many friends of Perry's considered Perry the best friend they ever had, they shared with us. Friends shared how much they loved and would miss Perry's hugs, his witty sense of humor, his intelligent debates and points of view.

Friends of Perry's we didn't even know shared fond memories. One friend later shared that Perry talked her out of suicide. We couldn't have known the impact Perry had on others here.

Other stories revolved around Perry's computer talent. He had been in high school honors computer classes and his teachers had shared with us, even before Perry passed, that they had never had a student so gifted with computers as Perry.

Perry had always been a strong visual learner. When he was three years old, he worked 100-piece puzzles. What impressed me most was the attention span this required from a three-year-old. At five years old, while the other kindergartners were drawing figurative images, Perry was drawing realistic 3D images of tables, chairs, houses, and other objects.

I shared with others Perry's love for astronomy in his younger years, and how he wanted to be an astronaut until one day, at five or six years old, he changed his mind. On our drive home from school, Perry asked me if astronauts can come home from work every day. I explained that they can't when they go on missions. He said, "I want to come home and see you and Daddy and Sissy and JoJo every day and have dinner . . . I think I'll be a mailman."

Perry started us off on a homeschooling journey when, as a gifted student in the second grade, he was in an inclusive classroom that was not a good match, and we didn't have school choice in the area we lived in.

Perry's mind was like a sponge. It was his heightened senses that allowed him to easily absorb information, but it was also his heightened senses that caused him to come home completely exhausted in first and second grade. Perry was a well-behaved student. He didn't act out; he just wasn't in a school environment that suited him well.

Perry homeschooled through eighth grade. There were pros and cons to homeschooling, but it turned out to be a good choice for our family. Perry thrived and his younger siblings did as well. We lived in an area with a decent amount of homeschooling support. Through programs and activities outside our home, and through individualized curriculums, I found that, beyond the mid-elementary years, I didn't need to teach my kids as much as I needed to facilitate their education. Homeschooling allowed me to plan according to each of my children's strengths and weaknesses.

The years really are short. It's the days of chaos—kitchen science experiments and read-alouds and art exploration and Lego towers and exploring in the dirt and even mishaps and unplanned messes—that contain my fondest memories. I have lived a life rich with so many extraordinary ordinary moments with my children. I am most grateful for all the creative and happy messes and memories we got to make together.

It was the ordinary moments, and not the trips or treats, that I cherish most about Perry's younger years. In fact, Perry disliked traveling, which made vacations a mixed bag for the entire family. He experienced car sickness, tension headaches, and migraines from the age of nine.

Perry had food sensitivities and physical sensitivities. He was very sensitive to cooking aromas. He disliked light touch but appreciated bear hugs. Perry liked to unwind by piling blankets on top of him. It was not an uncommon sight to find Perry under piles of blankets with bean bags piled on top of the blankets.

As his mom, I didn't wish that Perry wasn't so sensitive; I just wished that this world wasn't so loud, busy, chaotic, and insensitive. Neither was in my control, and I had to trust I was guiding Perry to the best of my ability.

I know everyone has some type of struggle, and I am aware these are not the heavy challenges that many others experience. Yet these were challenges Perry lived with, and they did affect our entire family at times. I am grateful he doesn't have to experience these issues now.

Perry's service turned out to be a beautiful tribute to him. Perry's friend Mahalia played her guitar and sang the most beautiful rendition of "See You Again" (Wiz Khalifa). Scout leaders and friends and family members spoke. The service lasted over two hours, and there was only standing room left. I remember seeing familiar faces in the hallway. Through all the endearing and funny stories each speaker shared, a theme emerged of how Perry was unassuming and quiet and intelligent, yet unexpectedly quick and brave and adventurous. And he always had to be a step ahead.

After the memorial, my sister-in-law Britta told me she had felt Perry's presence at the service. She didn't know Perry's friends, nor did she know of the close friendship he shared with Mahalia. Britta felt Perry's presence in an especially strong way while Mahalia sang, she told me.

Britta had previously shared with me and Craig that after

she received the news in Montana, she felt Perry close to her, passionately communicating he was sorry. This was sad to hear, yet it was what I needed to hear because it reassured me of what I wanted to believe but couldn't be certain of—nobody had hurt Perry.

We knew Perry's death was an accident—not murder or suicide—but that was all we knew for certain at that point. I was grateful Britta shared Perry's visit with us, for it gave me comfort amidst so many unknowns, during such an agonizing time.

We spent a week at my parents' house following the memorial. I spent most of this time in bed, in tears. Once while talking to my parents about how angry I was, I collapsed in a heap of tears over their kitchen island. When I broke down, I had been talking about how Perry didn't even have his wallet with him.

I sank into a crumpled mess on the floor. When I regained my composure, I stood up and turned to the fridge to get water. A note on the fridge door caught my eye that had been there all along, yet I hadn't noticed until this moment. It was written by Perry several months prior when Perry had gone to my parents' house to retrieve his wallet:

Hi, I had to get my wallet.

With Love,
—Perry

Above his handwriting was a scripture on the notepaper that read, "The wisdom from heaven is first of all pure." The magnet holding the notepaper read, "BE BRAVE & keep going."

9

My Past

I need to take you on a detour to share about my past spiritual experiences, for greater context and understanding of later chapters.

From as young as I can remember, when I heard news of one's passing, I immediately envisioned a scene around one's death. As a young child, I didn't give this any thought. As I got older, because I didn't otherwise have an overly active imagination, I began to chide myself for the random, morbid thoughts that made me feel I was obsessing over death. Ironically, these critical thoughts did lead me to obsess over death, but they never moved me any closer to understanding the true nature of the original thoughts.

When I was an older child, my dad told me that an out-of-town friend of mine had died in a car accident. Until I went to Carolyn's memorial service, I repeatedly saw flashes of moving images from inside a car window and other people around my friend Carolyn. I thought I was obsessing over her death, but I now know I was connecting with Carolyn in spirit, receiving impressions via shared thoughts. I had seen Carolyn's last vivid memory. It has only been over the past few years that I have come to understand this.

I reflect on the youngest days of my life and recall never feeling alone. Playing with my dolls or coloring or observing a bug on a blade of grass . . . before I even had the language to express it, I felt like God was with me, closer than a friend.

I have felt the presence of Christ, specifically, at certain times in my life—frequently in my young childhood, and as an adult. As a child, I felt the presence of what I now know to be angels. I can't recall connecting with any of my loved ones at a young age, but at that point I didn't have any loved ones in spirit.

I carry vivid early memories of playing with my dolls in my living room near a little round table and sensing other children with me. This didn't scare me. Either I assumed it was my imagination, or I assumed it was a normal experience everyone had. I didn't think much of it because I was so young and didn't know that others would have considered my experiences to be unusual.

I hadn't yet been taught what was normal, acceptable, godly or evil, so I was open and had no fear to limit or block such experiences from occurring. Many of my most content memories from childhood are from time spent alone, yet I never felt alone.

I was three years old when my brother Kevin was born. Before he was born, I had a memorable dream of floating above my mom and dad in their bedroom. I know the dream occurred before Kevin was born because I looked down at my mom who was sleeping and very pregnant. I saw everything in my mom and dad's room from a perspective of being above them. I knew I was a distance from my mom and dad, yet I felt happy and free and known from where I was.

I was born a pastor's daughter, raised in a Pentecostal denomination. I can appreciate my upbringing now for instilling in me a belief in (the holy) Spirit. I can't recall ever not believing in God as the unseen force of love more colossal than anyone, or any situation, here on earth.

Many people believe in God and are faithful to a church, yet many are cerebral in their faith, mistrusting of miracles and divine healing and other manifestations of the holy spirit. I wasn't raised in a church that was skeptical of modern movement of the holy spirit. I am grateful for having been raised with the belief that the holy spirit lives and breathes in and within our lives today.

The downside to my spiritual upbringing was strong opinions and expectations, man-made definitions, and specific, set beliefs regarding exactly how the holy spirit moves, who can be a conduit of the holy spirit, and what that looks and sounds like. Not necessarily what that feels like. I don't recall being taught to trust my intuition regarding these matters.

I came out of my childhood with a strong awareness of what others believed about the holy spirit. Any evidential move of the spirit outside the box of these beliefs would have been considered the work of the devil or evil spirits. My ministry today would not be accepted by the same denomination, simply because I do not place such limits on how the holy spirit serves through me.

I want to add that I didn't receive any personal or direct messages from my parents or anyone else in our church regarding these set beliefs. I received these messages through sermons, revivals, youth camps, and select media. My parents didn't preach to me at home; I was simply immersed in the culture.

Even though I don't carry such specific beliefs now, the beliefs of my childhood served to grow my faith as I came to trust in my own soul's knowing and personal relationship with God—a necessary precursor to the spiritual work I do now.

I never feared my spiritual experiences, but I feared what people would think about them. I feared what others would say about me if I expressed what fell outside their box of acceptable beliefs. I feared rejection. I didn't know it then, but fear was my barricade to receiving all that Spirit had for me to experience and share.

I was an older child when a respected, well-loved elder of our church passed away. My family and I were living in a parsonage that was literally attached to our church. We walked through our living room closet to enter the sanctuary. This gentleman's name was Robert Duty, but we referred to him as Brother Duty. His body was left in the sanctuary overnight, in preparation for his memorial service the next day.

The night before Brother Duty's service I felt very anxious, but I was a typical child in the sense that I found the situation creepy, as did my brother, and we fed each other's anxiety. I was getting ready for bed when I began seeing unfamiliar images in my mind.

I saw unique pieces of furniture and a lady I didn't recognize. The next day, at Brother Duty's service, the same lady I had seen in my vision was present, yet it was my first time meeting her. She was a relative of Brother Duty's from out of town. After Brother Duty died, his wife moved into a new house. While visiting his wife with my parents, I recognized furniture I hadn't seen in their former house. It was the furniture from my vision.

I had a minor surgery around the age of eleven, for which I was given light anesthesia. During the procedure I found myself floating at the top of the operating room. I could hear a faint hum coming from some piece of equipment on the opposite side of the room that was otherwise quiet.

I looked down upon two doctors. I had only met one of

the doctors prior to my procedure. Their conversation was relaxed, and I knew they were talking of weekend plans. Then I saw my body on the table. Medically speaking, the procedure went well. I didn't have a near-death experience, but I certainly had an out-of-body experience.

At the age of nineteen, I married after a whirlwind romance, just a few months after my enlistment in the US Navy had begun. My then-husband and I married eight weeks after meeting. Any assumption that our marriage was unhealthy, based on this information alone, would be correct.

After two years of marriage, my then-husband told me he was in love with me, as well as his girlfriend from high school. I had never really known grief until this point in my life, and I was devastated. Divorce held strong stigma in the church of my childhood, and lesser stigma within the church community I was involved with at the time. This stigma only added to my painful feelings of abandonment.

My husband and I were separated when, one desperate night, I cried out from our bedroom floor. I felt Spirit surround me and then Spirit prompted me to get my Bible. I opened my Bible to this very passage my eyes fell upon that I had never previously read:

"Do not be afraid; you will not be put to shame.
Do not fear disgrace; you will not be humiliated.
You will forget the shame of your youth
and remember no more the reproach of your widowhood.
For your Maker is your husband—
the LORD ALMIGHTY IS HIS NAME—
the Holy One of Israel is your Redeemer;
he is called the God of all the earth."

"The LORD *WILL CALL YOU BACK*
as if you were a wife deserted and distressed in spirit—
a wife who married young,
only to be rejected," says your God.
"For a brief moment I abandoned you,
but with deep compassion I will bring you back."

Isaiah 54:4-7

This experience was a spiritual awakening for me. It propelled me forward in my healing, helping me to release guilt and shame I had been carrying. I still mourned after that night and the divorce process was long and drawn out, but this was a turning point for me.

I began the process of forgiving my husband that night, and in doing so, I began to see my responsibility in my choice to marry and unloving behaviors I displayed in our marriage. I had previously blamed my husband, but this new clarity allowed me to see that I needed to forgive myself.

It took time, but I did come to fully forgive my then-husband and release all the pain from our marriage. I eventually lost my desire to be married to him, yet I wished for him to experience peace and a loving, happy future.

It was more than a year later when I was living in the single barracks again, enjoying friendships yet feeling frustrated because I wasn't yet divorced. I was feeling lost in confusion and frustration when, one night in bed, I prayerfully cried out for a sign.

The next morning while at work in the hospital lab, I wasn't thinking about my grievous state or prayer from the night before when I was introduced to the man who would become my best friend and future husband, Craig.

Craig and I were living off base in Waukegan, Illinois, when I had another memorable spiritual experience. We were both sailors, working the same shift and carpooling home together every afternoon. Craig was driving us home one day when, out of nowhere, I heard a male voice say, "I'm gonna die." Now, I should tell you that I didn't otherwise hear voices in my head, so this really stunned me. The voice was so loud that it seemed audible.

I immediately told Craig about this unusual experience. Then a car passed us, and I noticed the license plate: 2FAST4U. We rarely watched the news, but a week later we turned on the TV while eating dinner in our combined apartment dining and living room, and the news was on. A fatal car accident was being reported. A young man had died. The camera zoomed in on the license plate: 2FAST4U.

This was my first and only spiritual experience I had ever judged to be negative. For days, I wondered if I was somehow supposed to warn that young man, who was someone's son. This was before the age of Google. Could I have even accessed his information? If so, what would I, a stranger, have said? I couldn't figure out what I could have done to prevent the accident, but I was confused as to why I had the experience.

I don't believe this young man had a conscious awareness of his impending fatal accident, but I do believe his soul communicated with mine that day. I understand it now as a learning experience for me. Even the soul of a young man who died unexpectedly knew his time on earth was coming to an end.

Fast forward to 2000. Perry was two and Rayanna was a newborn when I had a dream visit from my mom. She was sitting in the corner of my room, and she looked to be in spirit. She said, "I'll always be with you." It was a loving experience, but I was scared when I woke up, and I called her immediately to make sure she was okay. I told her about the dream, and she shared with me how I had recently been in her dream as well.

The experience with the young driver and this experience with my mom have taught me it's not only the departed souls among us who can communicate. Our souls can and do communicate. This may more commonly occur in a dream state, when we get out of our own way, less tied to the physical realm and its lower energies.

We had just stopped trying to prevent pregnancy when Perry was conceived, and then Rayanna came along as a sweet surprise, just two years later, in 2000. In 2002, Craig and I felt as if our family was complete. We had been blessed with two healthy kids, a boy and a girl, just as I had always dreamed. Perry was four and tirelessly inquisitive. His mind and hands needed to stay active, which never really changed. Our nest was busy and full, and we were grateful.

One Sunday evening during this time, Craig was reading to the kids before bed with Rayanna curled up next to him and Perry playing at his feet. While I passed through to the kitchen, I noticed the TV was on in the far corner of our great room.

We don't keep the TV on as background noise, so this was unusual. The volume was low, and I couldn't hear what was specifically being said. I could see the show *Touched by an Angel* playing. Of course, right? I recognized Monica, the angel, and I could tell by the glow around her that she was in the enlightening moment reserved for the end of the program.

Angel Monica said "Jonas," the only word I heard. Not only did I hear the name, but *Jonas* reverberated in my ear, as if someone had spoken the name directly into my head. I had felt Spirit presence just before Monica said the name.

For me, feeling Spirit is like feeling a shift in the energy or air surrounding me. Unlike psychic vibes given off from people that may activate lower emotions within me, Spirit presence never feels negative or heavy. What Spirit presence feels like to me is electricity mixed with love. It's love with a charge.

I tried to articulate my *Jonas* experience to Craig. I wasn't sure myself what happened, but I told him what I felt certain of. I would soon be meeting someone named Jonas.

A few weeks later, I dreamt I was pregnant with a baby boy. I think it made Craig a bit nervous, so I reassured him I was sure it was just a silly dream. After all, I was on birth control pills and we were both happy with our family as it was, at least for the time being.

The following month I accompanied Craig on a work trip to Florida. My parents kept the kids while Craig and I enjoyed our first adventure sans kids since becoming parents. One evening while walking the beach, I shared with Craig what I just couldn't get off my mind.

I was having thoughts of what it would be like to have another baby. This was the first conversation we had where we both spoke fondly of having three children. We decided to stay open, and maybe even try, when the time felt right. It turned out that I was already pregnant with Jonas and just didn't know it yet.

Our mid-pregnancy ultrasound revealed I was carrying a boy. We decided Jonas would be our baby's name. I was selective with whom I shared his name story, and how I shared it. It was often simpler to say, "I had a dream." Over the years, I became quite adept at using this phrase to describe my spiritual experiences.

I wish I'd been braver in sharing back then, but I opted to take the simplest and most socially acceptable route. We all have dreams. I was just having waking dreams, too.

After Jonas was born, Craig called his parents in Montana to share the happy news. Craig told his dad, John, our baby's name. John expressed surprise and became emotional that we chose a family name. Craig was confused. Unbeknownst to us, Craig's grandfather Perry had a younger brother, Jonas, who had lived in Sweden. Even if Craig had heard the name in family discussion, it would have been pronounced "Yonas."

Craig was very fond of his grandfather Perry. Craig shared with me early on in our relationship how, shortly after his grandfather died, Craig walked into the living room, sat down, picked up a magazine and began reading it. Craig's friend asked how he was reading in the dark. At that moment, Craig noticed the room was dark, but he had previously seen it fully lit.

Grandfather Perry immigrated to the United States when he was seventeen. Our Perry was seventeen when he died. Like his grandfather, our Perry has a younger brother, Jonas.

When Jonas was a baby, I was doing laundry in the basement of our house while the kids were watching a kids' show in the adjoining family room. While folding laundry, Spirit presence washed over me. Suddenly I saw a flash of an image in my mind—a bouquet of yellow flowers wrapped with a red ribbon. The images weren't familiar to me, and I don't experience my own thoughts this way, as flashes popping in into my mind.

I went to turn off the TV and take the kids upstairs. Their show had ended, and *A Wedding Story* was playing, with a scene of a young lady walking on a beach. A young lady's voice was narrating that her sister had died in a car accident. Intrigued, I paused to watch more. The next scene showed the bride-to-be's wedding preparations. The bride-to-be stated she would be having yellow flowers in her wedding, in honor of her sister, whose favorite color was yellow. She would also wear a red ribbon of her sister's around her waist, she said.

I was thirty-three when I attended massage therapy school. I had earned my bachelor's degree in health care management years prior, while in the Navy, but there weren't any part-time or flexible jobs in my field where we lived. I wanted to contribute to the family income for the ongoing extras that life increasingly presented to a growing family.

The previous year I began researching schools or training I could attend that would accept my GI bill benefits, which would soon expire. I found a massage therapy school in our residential suburb. Intrigued, I considered that massage therapy might be flexible and rewarding work for me.

I was doubtful the school would accept the benefits, but I learned from the school website that they did indeed accept GI bill benefits. It worked out perfectly that my benefits covered enough for school and for me to hire my mom for part-time childcare. My mom was eager to help out and spend more time with her grandkids.

Toward the end of the massage therapy program, during clinic, I was working on a client's feet when I began to feel Spirit presence. I just figured my client was receiving healing that she needed. Then, a photographic image appeared in my mind of two little boys in a red wagon. I saw their hair color and the color of their clothing. This image disappeared and another image came to mind. This included one of the little boys in my previous mental image, but he appeared to be a little older and he was wearing a t-ball uniform. I saw the two-digit number on his t-ball shirt.

I wondered if I was reading my client's mind. I didn't know what was happening, but I certainly was not going to share my impressions with my client. A couple hours later, I saw another therapist at our lunch spot, and she began crying. I could hear her tell the other therapists how her friend, a young man, had died the previous night. Her friend had been battling terminal testicular cancer and was overwhelmed by excruciating pain when he died by suicide, she shared.

I felt an intense internal push that left me with no space to consider or question or let my nerves take over. I knew I had to share my experience with this grieving massage therapist. I told the therapist I had no idea if it would mean anything, but I had to share my experience with her. As I shared my impressions with her, her mouth opened wide and she told me I was describing the picture she had of her friend (who had died) with her boyfriend.

The following week, when I saw the therapist at work again, she told me she had relayed what I had shared with her to her deceased friend's parents. They told her the t-ball number I had seen in my vision was their son's t-ball number. She shared with me that her friend's parents received much comfort from my visions. She told me they belonged to a church that implied, by its doctrine, suicide is a sin. No wonder Spirit had pushed me to share.

My next story isn't about me, but I tell it to share how children are naturally very open to Spirit. Months after my massage therapy connection, my mom traveled to Indiana to help care for my aunt Mid as she neared the end of her battle with ovarian cancer.

During this time, I had many connections of feeling close to my family in Indiana. One morning I smelled bacon, only to find out later my mom had cooked a breakfast feast that morning. Another time, I smelled coffee while my mom and grandpa were enjoying a cup of coffee together. I also seemed to have an intuitive sense of how my aunt was feeling at certain times.

One day toward the end of my aunt Mid's life here, Rayanna was outside playing in the dirt, searching for ladybugs. She abruptly came inside and exclaimed, "Mommy, I just heard a noise outside that sounded like something died and came back to life!" I had never heard my little girl speak in such a way.

I called my mom. She told me that the previous day, the family had thought my aunt Mid was in her final moments. She had been sleeping a lot and was unresponsive for an extended period. On this day (the next day), to everyone's surprise, Aunt Mid woke up alert. Laughing and smiling, she enjoyed conversation with the family. Of course, my aunt Mid is more alive than ever, but from our earthly perspective, she had been dying and came back to life for one last get-together, and that was what Rayanna had sensed.

In 2012, I was serving in a volunteer role through our church for Interfaith Hospitality Network (IHN), a nonprofit agency that provides homeless families with housing and meals and job search assistance. As a family, at times we volunteered together, cooking and delivering dishes to various local host churches.

One evening during this time, I needed to attend a training at the local IHN office. As I was getting ready in my bathroom, I felt Spirit and saw a little boy in spirit to my left. He seemed to be sitting on my vanity and I felt as if he was watching me put my makeup on.

Then, an image of a beautiful woman with dark hair applying makeup came to my mind. In that moment, I understood that the little boy was watching this beautiful woman and not me, even though I didn't understand why I was having this experience.

I drove to the IHN office, listening to uplifting music on the Christian radio station and feeling Spirit presence the entire way there. I sat through the training and at the end, the woman who led the training said to me, "I'm sorry. I'm usually more enthusiastic than this." She went on to explain that her son had passed, and she was having a hard day. I looked at her. Although she was older than the image of the woman I had seen in my mind, she was beautiful and had dark hair, just like her.

I asked the woman how old her son was. I don't remember his age, but she told me he was an adult. I was confused but immediately experienced another moment of clarity—I had seen this woman's son as a little boy, and I had seen her through his eyes, through a memory from his childhood.

I told this beautiful mother, "I had a dream..." and I went on to share my experience with her. I recalled one more thing—the young boy did not seem to resemble his mother. I was curious and shared this with her. She told me that her son did not resemble her at all.

She shared with me that her son used to watch her get ready for work. Her son's spirit had felt so young and innocent, and there may have been another reason for this. She told me her son had been mentally disabled and had remained childlike throughout his life. No wonder he had appeared to me as a sweet little boy.

10

The Good in Today

A week after Perry's memorial in Tennessee, Craig and I felt it was time to go back to Ohio, even though we were not looking forward to our return. The morning we left for Ohio, my mom had a connection with Perry in a dream and she received a message she felt was for me: "Watch *Old Yeller* and drink a Dr Pepper!"

On our drive home, an idea came to my mind that I should look for the good in every day as a survival tool of sorts. I contemplated this thought while we traveled to Ohio. I decided I would look for the good in every day and share what I found on Facebook, where I knew I would receive support and encouragement.

This practice buffered my first horrendous weeks and early months of mourning. I couldn't do it every day, but when I could find something good in a day to focus on, for the few minutes it took to take a picture and share on Facebook, it helped.

Over time, this practice disproved my fear that life would always be horrible and painful, and it gave me a little respite from mourning. The practice caused me to pay attention, and by paying attention I discovered good moments, and more as time went on.

When we stopped at a gas station to refuel halfway between Tennessee and Ohio, we pulled up next to an acquaintance of mine from Tennessee! She gave our entire family tickets to a museum in Kentucky. After my mom's dream visit from Perry that morning and my own unexpectedly hopeful thoughts, this chance encounter and kind gesture signaled to me that heaven really was with us on this difficult day that marked time as moving forward without Perry. It was our first back-to-normal day, and these connections helped ease me back to Ohio.

Craig and Perry were the Dr Pepper drinkers, but I bought an old-fashioned glass bottle of Dr Pepper at the gas station. I saved it to drink with *Old Yeller* that night. When we returned to the townhouse, my entire core sank as I walked up the stairs and by his dark room. I missed Perry so deeply. I suggested to Craig that we sleep on Perry's sheets. Craig went into action immediately. He didn't just get Perry's sheets. He removed our mattress and replaced it with Perry's mattress.

As a family, on Perry's mattress with his unwashed sheets, we watched *Old Yeller.* We had watched it as a family several years before, so I had a fond memory of watching it with Perry. I surprised myself that I was able to focus on the movie, but I was eager to hear any messages from Perry in the movie. The ending quote really spoke to me:

> *"What I mean is, things like that happen. They may seem mighty cruel and unfair, but that's how life is a part of the time. But that isn't the only way life is. A part of the time, it's mighty good. And a man can't afford to waste all the good parts, worrying about the bad parts. That makes it all bad."*

Not only did this quote fill my heart, but I realized my own thoughts to look for the good in the day connected with these words from the movie! They had been inspired thoughts, from Spirit. I'm sure this had happened to me previously in life, and I'm sure this happens more than we realize, to all of us. Such thoughts come from God, and from no "place" other than heaven.

I saved my glass Dr Pepper bottle. Later, in a significant moment, the large numbers printed on the bottle—1024—would speak to me as an answer to a troublesome question—the time of Perry's death (or the time by which he could not have been rescued). Shortly afterward, the bottle would fall and break—the bottle, like the troublesome thoughts, no longer necessary to keep.

11

Finding Perry

After Perry's memorial, while still at my mom's house, I began to crave water and open space. Previously in life I had never experienced panic or extreme anxiety, but in the days that followed Perry's death, I found myself frequently sighing and my breathing was shallow. It had only been days, but I felt like I hadn't taken a deep breath since getting the news.

When I wasn't getting deep breaths, I was crying. I was suffocating in my anguish, choking on the pain my body was continuously releasing in those early days and weeks. I received many recommendations for antidepressants and anti-anxiety medications during this time. I was open to taking meds, but every time I considered it, my intuition told me medication wasn't for me.

I needed to feel the all of it, and I felt that I could only be present for my kids if I did not medicate. They were still growing, and I didn't want to miss out on more than was necessary for my healing. I trusted my decision was best for me, and the pain would eventually lessen. Now I can see how numbing my pain would not have been ideal for me, and it may have also numbed my discernment of Spirit.

I stayed open to changing my mind about medication, checking in with myself during hard periods of extreme mourning. I know this may not have been the ideal choice for someone else. It was simply the best choice for me, even though it meant having extreme anxiety for a limited time.

One week after we returned to Ohio and watched *Old Yeller*, my mom came to visit when Craig needed to return to work. I still craved open water and fresh air, so I booked a cottage on Lake Erie for us all to retreat to after Craig's first full week of work. It was on a Friday afternoon when we left for our weekend on the lake.

On the way to Lake Erie, I drifted off. I was in the state between waking and sleeping when I saw Perry. He appeared as if at the distant end of a long hallway, trying to get my attention. "Mom!" I heard and felt him passionately say, "Start it up!" He repeated this phrase.

I couldn't make sense of my experience. Not being able to understand what Perry had communicated only confirmed my rationalization: I wanted to see him so badly, my mind made up the experience. He was constantly on my mind, so it made sense I was now hallucinating. I believed Perry still existed, I believed heaven was among us, and I believed in my previous spiritual experiences and messages and signs. Yet I first looked for logical explanations.

Even so, the daydream left me with a sense of peace and comfort, and I wanted to believe Perry was talking about the blog I had thought about starting as something therapeutic for me to do. Blogging would be a way to journal and help me connect with others while I had this new difficulty in sustaining conversation. Maybe others would be inspired, and we would inspire each other. I wanted to understand Perry's message. What I really wanted was to believe my son truly had just connected with me.

We arrived at the cabin and immediately set our chairs up by the water. I breathed for what felt like the first time since Perry had died. We had a direct view of Cedar Point, the amusement park I had taken Perry to, across the lake. The cabin manager welcomed us and gave us a brochure for several different islands we could visit via ferry.

Craig and I could have spent the entire weekend just sitting at the water. We knew the kids would appreciate a little adventure, but I was anxious about facing a crowd and functioning in public. I perused the brochures; one contained information about Put-in-Bay and all its attractions, including "Perry's Victory and International Peace Memorial." I had to immediately show the family. Our plans were made for us; there was no question as to where we would spend our Saturday.

At our lake rental cottage, a train whistle woke me up early Saturday morning. Later the cabin manager apologized to us for the train whistle. She told us it wasn't typical, but a teenaged boy had recently been struck by a train here. He passed away, so the train was now blowing its whistle as it went by. Maybe this was supposed to be a warning for pedestrians, but Sunday morning when I heard the whistle again, it felt like a tribute.

Saturday morning we drove to the ferry that took us to the small island of Put-in-Bay. A little old radio sat on the counter of the first shop Rayanna and I walked into. "Wake Me Up When September Ends" by Green Day began to play when we walked in. This is the song Rayanna picked out for Perry's memorial service; it was a song Perry had introduced her to and not a song I had heard regularly on the radio.

We visited Put-in-Bay on the weekend commemoration for Commander Perry's birthday. "Perry" and "Don't Give Up the Ship" were plastered all over the small island. According to the sources at Put-in-Bay, Oliver Perry was a master commandant in the US Navy who led American naval forces into victory in a battle against the British Royal Navy. This was to gain control of the British-ruled Great Lakes (except for Lake Huron) at the beginning of the War of 1812.

Commander Perry was courageous and successful in battle, but a mosquito took his life. He died from yellow fever at the age of 34, on his birthday. Commander Perry is remembered for the words he scribbled on his battle flag, "Don't Give Up the Ship." This was a tribute to his friend and colleague who had died in battle, Captain James Lawrence of *USS Chesapeake*.

Not only did we see Perry's name everywhere, but things I read about Commander Perry reminded me of Perry. As we walked around, memories of Perry, and traits he was known and loved for, flooded my mind.

Perry seemed to be the least adaptable member of our family, but when the cards were down, he would shine. A deep sense of resilience and inner strength would rise to the top, surprising us all when times were tough. Perry had difficulty finding patience for minor disruptions, minutia, trivial concerns, and anything that didn't have sincere, worthy, or even reasonable motives behind it.

I admired Perry's fortitude, determination, and focus, but passion had to be a prerequisite for Perry to be so determined and focused. Perry was concerned with issues such as racism and equality, beyond his years, and if you needed someone to risk life and limb to save you, Perry would want to help.

I discovered another interesting connection. Commander Perry led naval troops into battle on September 10, which is my birthday. The synchronicities proved to me Perry was still around. That weekend gave me fresh air, room to breathe, and so much more.

During my mom's stay in Ohio with us, she and I took the

kids to a used bookstore and resale shop. Rayanna is passionate about books, and I wanted to give her as much time as she wanted to browse, but after fifteen minutes I felt myself begin to melt down. In these early days, when fatigue set in, my sorrow very quickly rose to the surface and I either cried or fought back tears. I fought back tears in the bookstore.

My mom stayed with Rayanna in the book section while Jonas and I walked the perimeter of the store. My mind went to our falling star and how I wished I had a picture of it. I had this thought, then we turned a corner and I saw a picture of the green aurora borealis in a night sky. I purchased the picture, unaware that it lit up, and we hung it inside our front door.

My mom and I also took the kids on a hike during her stay. I was surprised when we arrived to find at the entrance there was a sculpture of three children who appeared to be close in age and oldest to youngest, boy-girl-boy.

We enjoyed the hike and on the way back, a blue jay flew across my path, almost directly in front of my face. I thought about signs from heaven. *Isn't a cardinal supposed to be what our loved ones send?* As if on perfect cue, a cardinal flew across, directly in front of me.

12

Start It Up

Four days after my vision of Perry and his "Start it up!" message, I walked to Home Depot from our townhouse. I can't remember what my purpose was. I may have just been walking to walk. I remember exactly where I was in the store—walking past the key-making terminal in the paint department—when I suddenly felt Perry with me, on my left side.

As I left the store, I was overcome with the strongest sense of love and lightness I had experienced since Perry had died. I wanted to keep walking; I didn't want it to end. I returned to our rental townhouse and these feelings subsided.

A few minutes later, I felt Perry's presence again. I felt an internal prompting to visit a Facebook support group I had joined for bereaved parents, so I did. From there, one of the mothers, a friend I had made in the group, came to mind.

Kathryn and I had chatted quite a bit back and forth prior to this day. I knew that her son Kade was Perry's age, seventeen, and he had also recently passed. When I clicked on Messenger, I felt Perry say "Yes!" and then my "Start it up!" dream came to mind.

I told Kathryn about my experience and asked her if the phrase "start it up" meant anything to her, but she said it did not. Then, in her next message, Kathryn told me her husband (Kade's dad) was working on Kade's Jeep in their garage as we chatted. Kathryn messaged, "My husband is lying under it yelling at me to 'Start it up!'"

Of all the amazing, mind-blowing connections I have experienced since this day, this simple "Start it up!" from Perry and Kade to Kathryn and me will always be most spectacular.

13

Dream Visit

During my mom's stay in Ohio, my aunt Paulette and her friend Carol visited from Indiana. Their visit got me out of the house, and I welcomed their company. My aunt Paulette is also a bereaved mother to my cousin Megan, and Carol has experienced the death of her brother. They were both understanding and empathetic.

After my mom returned to Tennessee, I had to begin finding my way in a life that felt foreign. I felt displaced, but we weren't without support. A dear childhood friend, Chris, came to visit for a weekend, along with her three sweet boys. She took me shopping and cooked for us.

Craig and I found a support group and group counseling for the kids, but there may be such a thing as seeking this type of support too soon, at least for us. Our collective family memories of these experiences are not pleasant.

Perry's best friend and his dad spent a weekend with us at the close of summer. My mom returned with my cousins—Nichole, Angela, and Jennifer—for a weekend that brought us a little joy. Over the course of a year, the days that we had company after Perry's death totaled over six months. That's a lot of support and love from friends and family.

As the summer ended, I felt lost, empty, skeptical, and

even fearful of how we could possibly start over again. I couldn't bear the thought of staying where we were, yet I was exhausted, and I couldn't imagine moving. Grief depleted me. By this point, I was certain Perry was only on the other side of the veil that separates us, but what you need to know is this:

The connection with Perry I had experienced made Perry's physical death even more real to me, and in the first few months, this was a very painful reality to accept. Seeing my son in spirit didn't allow me to experience denial that Perry was not here in body.

Nor did my connection with Perry in spirit swiftly teleport me to emotional acceptance of his death. My son was alive, and he was dead. I found him, and I had lost him. My son had graduated from his earthly journey, and my baby was gone. My pain was still raw.

Yes, I had moments of pure, loving, spiritual connection like I had never experienced. Most of the time, though, I felt like a burn victim walking around outdoors in a sandstorm. I had lost my identity. I had lost one of my babies. *Mother* was the earthly role I most identified with and cherished.

I had no doubt we are spiritual beings, living here temporarily, learning lessons and all. I got that, but it would take a long time and much release for my heart to adjust. I missed our physical connection, and I mourned this long after I knew Perry was closer than humanly possible.

One day while we were still living in Ohio, Jonas and I walked to the nearby park with the water tower. The last time Jonas had been there was with Perry. The last time I had been there was searching for Perry. At the park, Jonas told me how Perry had tossed his hacky sack around with him, teaching him different tricks. I could feel and hear the pain in Jonas's voice as he choked up reliving the memory.

As we walked back toward our townhouse, Jonas saw a shopping cart ahead of us. He pointed it out, obviously surprised by it. I had never noticed a shopping cart on the sidewalk while living there, but it wasn't something crazy unusual, either. Then Jonas shared the significance with me.

He had just been reminiscing about a recent time when he, Perry, and Rayanna found a shopping cart while walking at this same place.

The kids found the shopping cart and Perry wanted to push one of his siblings in it, but they declined his offer. "Okay, push me!" Perry yelled as he got in the cart. Running, Rayanna and Jonas pushed Perry along as Perry yelled, "Faster, faster!" They all laughed their way back home.

When Jonas and I returned home from our walk that day, I told Rayanna about the shopping cart and she went outside to see it. I took a picture of Rayanna and Jonas by the shopping cart. A man walked by, and to this day I chuckle when I think about what he must have thought!

Around this time I met Cindy, whose son Zach had recently passed. One night, he came to me in a dream wearing a sleeveless blue t-shirt that looked too small, yet he was beaming as he flexed his muscles and flashed a contagious smile! Zach told me he was okay in heaven. He said, "I'm Yippee Skippee... Yippee Skippee Skipperton!" This made me laugh. I later asked Cindy if Zach was funny, and she said he was. He is funny, and Cindy told me this is something her fun-loving Zach would have said here, too.

Cindy shared with me that she and her husband were preparing for a trip to Las Vegas. This was a vacation spot they loved to go with Zach, but this would be their first trip without him. After the trip, Cindy told me she rode the zipline, and I had no doubt Zach was with his mom. I could hear him again, yelling, "Yippee Skippee Skipperton!"

I could definitely see Zach and Perry becoming fast friends in heaven!

Shortly after the shopping cart experience, I had a dream visit from Perry while taking a nap in the middle of the day. The experience felt so real that when I first awoke, I didn't realize it had been a dream.

Perry was wearing the Vans, beige skinny jeans, and t-shirt he had worn on the day of our Cedar Point trip when I saw him standing in front of me, smiling. "Mom," he said. Then he hovered directly above me, his body parallel to mine, and his eyes looked directly into mine. We were as close as we could possibly be without touching. Next, I felt the weight and warmth from his bear hug. Electricity mixed with love coursed through my veins. Overwhelmed, I began crying.

"You loved me so, so well!" he said. Perry's hug lingered for several moments longer. I woke up and could no longer see Perry, but I could still feel the warmth and pressure of his body. I touched my face and felt the wet tears I had cried.

This was the embrace I had been longing for.

14

Moving Forward

As fall approached, I began to fear winter and not being able to get outside and walk. Intense grief had stripped me down to survival mode. I was living one day at a time, and daily walks had become my lifeline. The walks kept me going, but it was also becoming increasingly painful to walk so close to where our son died.

I also had difficulty being out at dusk and after dusk. This aftereffect of the trauma would continue for many months. This wasn't hard to manage because I was exhausted and in my pajamas at or by five o'clock anyway, ready for bed. Eventually I would face my fear, but it would take months. Now I don't give a second thought to taking a sunset walk or going out at night.

Living where we had overwhelming trauma yet no friends or family had us all feeling displaced and isolated, but also open to just about anything else! Craig came home from work one day and rattled off several cities throughout the US. He asked me what I thought about moving to one of these cities. He'd been offered a position with Wells Fargo.

He had me at Phoenix. All I could see was taking a walk in the sunshine, and that thought almost felt good. In our grievous state of just living to get through each day, we didn't overthink. We no longer needed the rest of our lives or even the next five years to be planned out. We needed to get through the winter. Craig was on board with Phoenix. I knew the kids would be on board, and they were.

I'm not sure how we had the strength to pack up and move, but we did. No doubt heaven helped us! I was grateful our kids were older and self-sufficient. We had booked a cruise for fall break, and we decided to keep our plans. The timing worked out perfectly. We would pack up our townhouse, go on our cruise, and then head west in time to find a place to live, before Craig would have to start his new job.

We put off Perry's room to pack last. When I began packing the day before we moved, I found his watch between his bed frame and the wall. Perry's friend Ronnie had given Perry his watch as a birthday gift, and Ronnie wore one just like it. When I found Perry's watch it had stopped on 11:11:11.

That night we went out to dinner. On the way to the restaurant, Jonas was chatting with Rayanna when I heard him say, "one-one-one, one-one-one." I hadn't yet told the kids about Perry's watch, only Craig. Surprised, I asked Jonas what he was talking about. He said he was talking about the release date for Perry's favorite game, Skyrim.

We returned home and I finished packing Perry's room alone while Craig watched a movie with Jonas and Rayanna. This was my second most painful night in Ohio. I thought about Ronnie telling me what Perry had told him the weekend before he died: "Perry told me about the house you looked at. I could tell he was considering Ohio home."

I cried myself to sleep on Perry's bedroom floor that evening. When I woke up, I went into the kids' bathroom. It was empty. I opened the cabinet doors and drawers to make sure the kids had packed up everything. The bathroom was empty, except for one large goose feather on the bathroom closet floor.

As we drove away from our townhouse the next morning, I felt a weight being lifted from me and I knew this was more than a fleeting feeling. I was experiencing an emotional release. And I had my feather to remind me Perry traveled with us. We weren't leaving him behind.

What I left behind was an ocean of tears and pain. As we merged onto the highway that morning, the song that Rayanna picked out for Perry's memorial, "Wake Me Up When September Ends," began playing in my head. It was the end of September.

Craig and I found ourselves grateful for small accomplishments we previously wouldn't have thought anything of. The paradox was that we felt shit on by a cruel universe, yet we became more grateful. Every day we were grateful to make it through another day. I made it through my birthday. We got the townhouse packed up. Craig finished his paperwork for his new job. I cooked a meal. School arrangements were made.

It was time for a vacation. The cruise was ideal because the kids would have their own activities while Craig and I were able to sleep, rest, or mourn in the cabin without dragging each other down.

Our first cruise excursion was a guided bus tour in Puerto Rico. A friendly couple sat in the row in front of us on the bus. They appeared to be our age. The husband was sitting by the window with his body propped toward us, his arm bent on the seat. He looked back a couple of times, smiling. This told me he was planning to chat.

I felt my chest tighten as I worried that this man would ask us how many kids we had. Or maybe he would tell us how happy he and his wife were to get away from their kids. I worried about losing my composure that hung so loosely by a thread in my early days of grief.

The friendly man asked us where we were from, then he asked our kids how old they were. Thankfully, he did not ask us if we had other kids. A saving grace was that, outwardly, we were the ideal family—a family of four with a boy and a girl. I can't recall anyone asking us if we had other kids when we've been together. A family of four is the American dream, but our heartbreak.

The man told us we had a lovely family. What he said next took me by surprise. He shared that he and his wife had always wanted kids, but they were never able to conceive. At this point we had to exit the bus for our first leg of the tour. He and his wife followed us, and he began chatting with Jonas. He commented that Jonas had a good sense of humor, and he seemed to enjoy engaging Jonas in conversation.

Back on the bus, the man continued to share with us how they had wanted to adopt children, but every attempt fell through. I saw longing in his eyes as he looked at our children, but his tune quickly changed as he continued sharing. He and his wife got involved with youth ministry at their local church, he told us.

I don't remember the man's exact words, but he expressed that while life didn't turn out how he and his wife had planned, they had a good life. He said this with a smile, and I felt genuine gratitude behind his words.

How odd it was that this man had shared such an intimate story with us, strangers on a crowded bus. Craig and I were certainly not conversational that day and hadn't prompt him to share.

Earth angels come in all forms, and this man was one for me. He shifted my perspective. I had been resentful of others who never had to go through what we were going through.

The man on the bus admired our family. He saw the family and the love we had been blessed with ... not what we had lost.

This man on the bus opened my eyes to see that we all carry crosses. This was a perspective I had lost when Perry died. Pain is pain, and comparison of our pain is not a worthy pursuit. Comparison divides us, it never unites us.

I stopped ranking pain and started relating again. I began moving forward in healing as we began moving forward in a new life.

It's not the cross, but how we choose to carry it, that determines how we feel.

15

Arizona

I can't express enough gratitude for my mom. Traveling with us across the country in October, she helped us move, find a rental, and get settled in. She stayed with us through Craig's birthday in early November. We had never been to Phoenix. We drove into the city late at night with all our belongings, including a cat, a Russian tortoise, Stan the hedgehog, and Perry's cactus.

Shortly after we had moved into our townhouse in Ohio, Perry and Rayanna went to Home Depot to pick out plants. How appropriate it is now that Perry picked out a cactus. I almost killed it in transit, but it survived . . . just a little broken. We would put it on our patio in Arizona, where its new growth would quickly form a heart shape.

Our first stay in Phoenix wasn't at the best motel in the best part of town, but thankfully that wasn't a sign of things to come, and we laugh about the experience now. After our first full day in the Phoenix area, we checked into an Extended Stay in Mesa, hauling in our tribe and temporary living needs. I experienced mixed emotions in our new surroundings.

I couldn't see new, unfamiliar terrain without knowing Perry would never see it with us, and my heart ached. Every new sight and experience brought with it these same feelings, for many months.

I knew Perry was experiencing life with us in a different way. I knew he wasn't missing out, but there is no spiritual quick pass through grief. Spiritual awareness didn't escort me to the front of the healing line. My broken heart needed time to align with what my soul already knew.

The paradox of the heart is that it can carry different emotions together. I grieved the places Perry would never see with human eyes, but the same new experiences reintroduced me to hope, and even a bit of excitement. I experienced a welcomed feeling of newness and openness, despite my sorrow.

We ate at new restaurants and walked around exploring new grocery stores. We even cooked a couple meals in the kitchen of our hotel room. A relative set us up with a realtor who showed us rentals.

My mom gave me a book she had brought with her and wanted me to read. I expressed unease about reading a grief book while sharing a hotel room with my family and subjecting them to more mourning. This was a book unlike any other grief book she had read, my mom reassured me. I read Tom Zuba's *Permission to Mourn—A New Way to Do Grief* over the course of two days. I reread it later, aloud, to Craig.

I'll never forget where I was when I first read Tom's book because I will never forget how I felt as I read it—held by Spirit. Many times, I felt Perry by my side as I read the book. Once, I put the book down to go to the grocery store, and I felt as if Perry was still right beside me in the store—in the same way I had felt him with me in Home Depot.

Perry's presence told me I was supposed to be reading this book. Tom's words were truth my soul recognized and salve my heart needed.

At the end of our first week in Mesa, we found a rental house in Chandler. I drove my mom and kids to our new home. We went in and walked through, and then we gathered in the dining area. I sat on the tiled floor under the kitchen island and a tiny down feather slowly drifted downward (apparently from the underside of the kitchen island), landing on my lap, as if on perfect cue. I showed my mom, who knew about my feather from our Ohio move.

We were both so grateful for what we immediately recognized as a sign from heaven. It was a perfectly, divinely timed message that just as Perry had traveled with us, he arrived with us. Unlike us, he traveled light and easy. In all ways.

16

Doing My Part

The move and settling into our new home didn't take away my grief, but it did provide distraction that was respite from painful thoughts I could otherwise fixate on. An additional blessing was sunshine. We had moved at the perfect time of year, October.

Winter's promise of sunny days with lots of new places to explore gave me reason to feel hopeful. There was a lovely park in our subdivision just a few steps from our rental home. It became easy for me to make myself go for a daily walk.

Taking a walk became my daily goal. I couldn't do it every day, and at times I had to push myself, but I did it enough that walking became routine. Even during my most difficult times, I could only feel so bad while walking. I walked to clear my head. I walked to release. I walked to pray. I walked to feel okay.

I knew that no matter what emotions came up on any given day, for thirty minutes or so, I would be okay. Walking sorted out confusing thoughts and it released painful emotions. When I was cried out, walking helped me release more. I began to feel all right for a day at a time, and I believe walking made this possible sooner rather than later.

I walked with the kids and I walked with Craig in the evening, but it was my alone time spent walking that was so therapeutic for me. If I had difficult emotions to process, walking outside provided a supportive place for me to do so. Moving my body kept me grounded. I could devote my full attention to my emotions without being taken under by them. Walking helped me make sense of things and helped me see when things weren't making sense—when grief had taken over and caused my thoughts to become irrational. Over time, my walks helped me shift from being consumed by my grief to becoming an observer of it.

At the time, I didn't recognize these benefits of walking. I was just walking because it felt like survival. It sounds too simple, even naïve when comparing walking to my spiritual experiences. Yet walking played a considerable role in my healing. Ongoing healing could only result from doing simple things for my highest good, repeatedly.

My spiritual experiences have been more healing than I can even know. Spirit gave me the keys, but it was up to me to use them. I could open the next door and continue walking forward. Not even heaven could do this for me, but with every new step I took in the direction of healing, Spirit encouraged me with signs and presence.

Tom Zuba's book was a key to healing. After reading Tom's book I found his website, and in November I signed up for his "Living WITH the Holidays" grief support program. I am grateful for Tom's guidance during this time, and I am grateful for friendships made through Tom's program. As Tom might say, I am glad I said yes.

Around this time, I joined the local rec center and began attending yoga classes. I received so many signs from Perry on my way to class and while in class. This encouraged me to keep it up. I added Zumba and later began to occasionally attend evening line dance classes. I didn't push myself, especially in the evening when I was typically exhausted.

I didn't try to create a daily or weekly workout plan. I

didn't have the energy or motivation or focus to do so. It would be close to a year from this point that I would feel enough internal drive to push myself again. Until then, my healing came from questioning what I should do in the present moment, and just doing it.

Even though I couldn't consistently attend fitness classes, I did make them a priority in my life. I noticed that yoga improved my anxiety and shallow breathing, and if I missed a week, both returned. I noticed my grief was heavier and more intense when I went more than a couple days without moving my body. I began taking daily Epsom salt and essential oil baths. I noticed every single thing that made me feel better, and I slowly built upon those behaviors and activities.

Most significant to my overall wellness and healing may have been that I allowed myself to say no to anything that didn't feel good, and I didn't allow myself to feel guilty about it.

Being in a new place without family and long-term friends was lonely at times, especially during the holidays. Yet there was a blessing in our circumstances, and it was huge: My family and I didn't have social obligations or expectations. It was easy for us to make choices based on what felt good to us, individually and as a family. We didn't have much we needed to say no to.

I took care of myself like I had never taken care of myself before, like the rest of my life depended on it. Good support encouraged me to take care of myself, but support couldn't have substituted for self-care any more than it could have substituted for mourning.

Healing was a balancing act for me. I had to feel all the pain, yet I had to focus on that which made me feel better. I had to be gentle with myself, yet I had to make myself move. Waves of grief knocked me over, and I let them. Healing asked that I simply breathed through the pain, and when the waves subsided, I got back up and walked. Literally and figuratively.

17

Need to Know

"A boy, before he really grows up, is pretty much like a wild animal. He can get the wits scared clear out of him today and by tomorrow have forgotten all about it."

Fred Gipson, *Old Yeller*

Perry was running or walking when he fell less than a quarter of a mile from our townhouse. He never got back up. He most likely fell shortly before this because he had other minor injuries, in addition to the head injury that is thought to have been incurred from losing consciousness. Perry's body also had minor abrasions, and these were more alarming to me because they could signify being harmed or putting up a fight. There was no evidence to indicate Perry had been harmed, which reassured me.

Two months after the autopsy, the toxicology report came back negative, except for caffeine. This did not surprise us, but I knew there was more we didn't know. I knew Perry wanted to take responsibility for what we didn't know, and I knew mischief was involved.

When I could convince myself he wasn't harmed, I could

fathom Perry climbing on the farmhouse and accidentally falling. That would have been like him (to climb, not fall), but his body was found too distant from the farmhouse, closer to the adjoining property.

Falling from his bike onto gravel or asphalt was a greater likelihood, consistent with Perry's injuries and marks on his clothing. A fall from his bike would not have been likely to cause fatal injury, but the extent of his injuries could not be certain given the time that had passed before his body was found.

The caffeine came more into question as causing internal injury. We found an energy drink can after his death. It was at the location Perry would have been while talking to his friends before dinner, Monday evening. There was liquid left in the can, so he didn't drink it all.

Later, we would have more information that explained how Perry could have died from seemingly minor injuries, but for a long time this did not seem plausible. Another question left unanswered was whether Perry could have gone to a different location before ending up at the farmhouse property. He could have gotten picked up and dropped off (alive) at the property, or he could have made his way there after falling off his bike on or near the road.

Regardless of where he went when he left home, Perry was most likely trying to make it back home when he died. An unopened bottle of Visine eyedrops was found in his bike pouch. Later, a friend of Perry's shared with me that Perry took 25I-NBOMe that night, and I shared with the detective.

25I-NBOMe is also known as 25I or N-BOM. It is a synthetic LSD heavily marketed online to youth and commonly passed around at high school and college parties. The detective ordered for Perry's blood to be tested for 25I and then we had to wait for those results. We had already moved from Ohio when we got the results that LSD was detected in Perry's system.

Psychedelic drugs are not something Craig or I were familiar with. We did know of the dangers. I knew LSD was a hallucinogenic drug. I knew that people could die from accidents after taking the drug, due to being out of touch with their physical environment. In fact, just a week or so before Perry died, we had a conversation about LSD and this very topic. I don't believe this was a coincidence.

LSD is taken to experience different levels of consciousness. The irony is not lost on me that my son's intent was to have some sort of fun, even enlightening, psychic experience, and now I have psychic experiences.

Many teenagers are aware of 25I. It is not an addictive drug, and most who take it experience no ill effects. Most parents have never heard of 25I. Those who take 25I consider it LSD and believe it to be harmless. LSD is not known to cause harm, and deaths related to LSD do not result from the drug itself.

25I's primary ingredient is LSD, but other chemicals are mixed with it, giving it an unstable chemical structure, unlike LSD. When it comes to deaths associated with 25I, like LSD, most are injury related, but the injuries tend to be less severe than injuries sustained by LSD users. It has become known that fluid is found around the heart of injury victims who had consumed 25I.

Fluid was found around Perry's heart. This created even more questions before we knew of his 25I consumption. We had focused on the caffeine consumption and considered testing for unknown cardiac issues Perry may have had. Fluid around the heart occurs because 25I is a dangerous vasoconstrictor, making it less likely that one can survive otherwise minor or non-fatal injury after ingestion.

Caffeine is also a vasoconstrictor. No doubt Perry had kept the energy drink out of my sight because he knew I felt energy drinks were dangerous. We have learned from the police that it is not uncommon for teenagers to mix cold medicine, ADHD meds, and various prescription or over the counter (OTC) drugs with energy drinks to create a party drug or hallucinogenic effect, but the energy drink Perry had consumed had nothing else in it, nor did Perry's system have any of these substances in it.

Of the young people in spirit I have connected with who had consumed OTC, prescription, or recreational drugs not known to be harmful, energy drinks have been a correlation in most of their deaths.

I have no doubt that drugs not known to be harmful are responsible for more sudden deaths and accidents involving young people than we realize. Recreational, OTC, and many prescription medications may go undetected as a factor because they are not likely to be included on a standard toxicology panel. I obviously know this through my own experience, and I am more aware because I have heard similar stories from other people. I am regularly shown this information from a different view as well, through memories of the departed.

One must request to have such drugs specifically tested for. Consider that most young people who die after taking such drugs are not regular drug users, so their loved ones are not likely to even know what to ask for. Also, there is a limited window of time that postmortem testing can be performed.

After Perry's toxicology screen for 25I came back positive for LSD, I googled 25I and became sick to my stomach sifting through what I found. I scrolled through and watched snippets of a plethora of YouTube clips. Articulate, professional-looking young adults explained how safe 25I is. They gave tips for best practices in using it and how one might experience various levels of consciousness by taking 25I.

The young adults in these videos could have been graduate students or young professionals talking about B-complex vitamins and their long-term benefits. These healthy-looking spokespeople did not represent specific (illegal) companies but shared several websites as "reputable providers" for 25I.

Perry was daring but he could be conscientious. His friends shared with me that Perry wouldn't have consumed anything he wasn't aware of, nor anything he felt to be harmful. Earlier in the summer, prior to Perry's death, I read a conversation between Perry and one of his best friends. Perry told his friend he didn't want to take up cigarettes. "I don't want to get addicted and get lung cancer," he had typed to his friend.

I personally feel that postmortem toxicology screening should be expanded to include more substances. We owe this to bereaved families who should be provided with as much information as can possibly be detected up front. In the absence of serious injury, unknown substance-related deaths are too often attributed to Sudden Arrhythmic Death Syndrome (SADS).

I am aware that people die innocently from SADS, in the absence of external factors, from unknown cardiac issues and other chronic health conditions. And a person can die from a head injury alone. Life is not an action movie where people survive injuries our bodies are not made to survive in real life. A concussion alone can cause aneurysm or death, even in a healthy young person, particularly when exertion and heat are factors.

Yet with cases of SADS where substance use is an undetected factor, this creates unnecessary health worries for surviving siblings and their parents. Before we received the 25I results, Perry having undetected cardiac, seizure, or other disorder was a concern we had for our surviving children.

Answers can help family members move out of living in the trauma of their loved one's death. When we don't have answers, it is easy to obsess over a loved one's final moments.

My experience and my work have taught me that fears and imagined scenarios are often worse than the true circumstances around a love one's passing, and for this reason, answers can help families move forward in their healing.

When we can't get answers through physical evidence or

testing, evidential mediumship may serve us well. We may never know all the details surrounding a loved one's passing. We have unknowns around our son's passing. In Perry's case, we believe several factors came together to create a perfect storm he could not survive, with 251 being the primary factor. We do not know how heavily each of the additional factors weighed.

And when we can't learn all the facts through physical means or mediumship, Spirit can help us surrender the unknowns. Spirit showed me that surrender meant letting go of the rope I had been so tightly gripping. I could continue to grip, but only in exchange for inner peace. If I continued to grip, I would be trading my inner peace for an external outcome that was not even close to the reality Perry now lives in.

Once I began to loosen my grip, I began to live with a sigh of relief. In the end, I knew Perry wasn't scared when he took his last breath. I knew he didn't suffer. I knew he didn't want others to carry guilt for his choice. I love him no less by allowing him to accept responsibility for his choice. In fact, I honor my son, his story and journey, by doing so.

I want to express one more insight Spirit has taught me regarding physical death. Our perspective of a loved one's death, regardless of known or unknown factors, is worse than what a departed loved one experiences in death. God rescues a soul before experiencing extreme pain, and hearts can keep beating long after a soul is enveloped in God's radiant love and light.

18

Blame

I realize my story may read like a roller coaster, up and down. Maybe this means I have accurately portrayed a glimpse into what my first year after Perry's death was like, even though I would love for it to read more smoothly.

Before and after we had answers, I sought to practice forgiving every potential scenario that may have occurred, and involvement anyone else may have had, concerning Perry's passing. I imagined worst-case scenarios through a lens of how I might ever be able to forgive. This began with a desire to release, to forgive. I had a lot of emotions to work through in order to find this desire.

Anger was tied to my sorrow, and I released mostly through tears. At first, I was angry at Perry because he knew better. But he died. I had no idea who made, marketed, and sold the miniscule amount of 25I that my son ingested, but I hated them. I hated that they would never know the devastating consequences of their actions.

Then, I was angry at all the teens who take 25I, or any drug, and walk away. I was angry at stories of teens being reckless and surviving. I was angry that I survived all my stupid choices, but my son did not.

I was angry at parents who don't know or care where

their children are. I didn't want other kids to die and I didn't want other parents to feel my pain. I was just angry at life for being what it is—unfair. I was angry at a cruel and uncaring universe.

I was angry at all the kids who never have to admit to their reckless behavior. I was angry at the hiding. I was angry that 99% of young people's close calls and reckless stories will stay private. I was angry that we leave authenticity and hard lessons for the dead to share.

I was angry at the pharmaceutical industry and our culture that glorifies reaching outside of ourselves for something to make us feel better. I was angry at how, as adults, we model this behavior all too well.

I was angry at God. I had experienced God's presence in a strong way, but this didn't take away my anger. I struggled with reconciling the knowledge that angels had surrounded us since Perry had died, while understanding that angels didn't spare my son's life. I spent many nights on the floor in guttural cries asking God, "WHY?" Why wasn't Perry worthy to be saved, when so many others obviously were?

The person I was most angry at was myself. I couldn't find Perry. I didn't stop him that night. I didn't make different plans that day. I didn't snoop on his phone calls. I didn't rescue him. I didn't scream at the cops. I didn't do what I felt I was born to do—protect my child from harm. I wanted someone to pay and it was easy to blame myself.

Craig experienced the same feelings, but we never blamed each other. We only saw in each other the ways we had loved and parented Perry well. I'm not sure what came first, but when I felt forgiving of myself, I slowly came to feel forgiving of others. I traveled a long path of intention, focus, and release to reach that place.

What others may not understand about parental grief is that we don't have to be responsible for our child's death to blame ourselves. Regardless of how a child dies, parental guilt is something most bereaved parents have held at one time or another. Too many never let it go.

I held myself most responsible for Perry's death. Intellectually, I knew I wasn't, but my heart carried the guilt. I was Perry's guardian and I wouldn't experience lasting peace until I could forgive myself for what I thought I should have or shouldn't have done. My thoughts didn't have to be true or logical or reasonable, yet I had to honor them because the feelings they produced within me were real.

I convinced myself I wasn't strict enough with Perry. Then I recalled boundaries and expectations Perry was fully aware of and honored, even when he wasn't happy about them. Then I convinced myself I was too strict, until I recalled that I was not, and then again, I convinced myself I wasn't strict enough. This was a circular argument with myself I could only lose.

I pondered what I did too much of and too little of. I wondered what I missed. Surely, I overlooked one of the to-dos on the checklist of parenting, or else this wouldn't have happened.

We had all the big talks with Perry. We went beyond "Don't do this or that." At times, this embarrassed Perry and us, but we asked questions and sought to understand Perry's deeper thoughts on awkward and difficult topics.

When Perry was close to seventeen, he shared with me that an older brother of his friend had gotten a DUI. We discussed not riding with others who had been drinking alcohol. I asked him what he'd do himself if he drank away from home. This was an awkward conversation because I had no reason to believe Perry had tried alcohol, but at his age I knew drinking would be a temptation if it hadn't yet been.

When Perry's friends came over, we put the alcohol in our bedroom to remove temptation. If he and his friends wandered our property, Craig or I conveniently wandered into the kitchen when they came back in, getting close enough to chat, to get a good whiff. They didn't give us reason to suspect any substance usage.

I had talked to Perry about the danger of energy drinks many times. A year or so prior to Perry's passing, a local high school football player died unexpectedly. Energy drinks were associated with his death, so we discussed energy drinks again. Energy drinks scared me early on because they are so socially acceptable and available.

Perry had consumed energy drinks at various youth outings, and for the longest time, he was small for his age. I worried during these events that he would consume too much caffeine without eating or drinking enough. As a small fourteen-year-old at a teen event, Perry might follow the lead of an eighteen-year-old double his weight.

We had talked about the dangers of addictive drugs, about how they altered one's brain chemistry in such a way that addiction resulted.

I reassured myself by recalling the discussions we'd had, but new should-haves, what-ifs, and reasons to blame myself cropped up as time went on. As mother to Perry, I hadn't lived with respect and understanding of my own spiritual strengths. I didn't teach this to my children. I couldn't teach them what I didn't know at the time, but this was still a painful consideration.

What if I had known I could have received spiritual guidance on the night Perry died? What if Perry came to me because I could have saved him? These were my most painful what-ifs, yet I have made peace with them. I no longer live in a space of what-ifs, and the questions themselves are no longer relevant to me.

I have surrendered my old belief that it was my job to save Perry from his death. I never had that much power. Even today, my mind could hop on the what-if train, but I allow my spirit to direct my thoughts.

19

External Validation

In November, someone sent me a text with a beautiful poem. I felt Spirit with me as I read the poem. The author's name was Fara Gibson. I googled her name and found her website. I learned Fara was a psychic medium and she lived in Gilbert, Arizona, which was our neighboring town! Intrigued, I perused her site and noticed an upcoming group reading at a local yoga studio.

I had never seen a medium, and to be honest, the thought of seeing one made me nervous. I didn't fear evil presence. I trusted my intuition and God's protection. I was afraid of added disappointment. My concern was that it wouldn't work, and I would get no validation of Perry's presence. At four months along in my grief journey, I couldn't handle added heartache. I was mourning enough and didn't want to bring added grief upon myself.

I hadn't been thinking of seeing a medium, yet I felt Spirit, and the likelihood that the first medium I looked up would live nearby seemed more than coincidental. I asked Craig for his thoughts. He had no interest in going himself, but he took no issue with me going to Fara's group reading.

The fee for Fara's group reading was due in cash at the door, so I didn't have to commit ahead of time. I decided to trust what I felt led to do the day of the reading. When the day arrived, I woke up feeling Spirit around me. This was my assurance. I made plans to attend.

I felt Spirit presence very strongly during Fara's two-hour event. I appreciated listening to all the healing validations and loving messages Fara so evidently brought through for others in attendance. At the very end of the reading, Fara came to me and described a teenaged boy in spirit who was, without a doubt, Perry.

I received many validations, including specific details around Perry's passing that confirmed what I had intuited but didn't have evidence for. These details came through in a way that I knew was from Perry. I didn't believe that Fara was reading my mind or energy, nor was there any way she could have possessed knowledge of these details.

I had experienced connections with my son, but mediumship served me in a way that I couldn't and can't serve myself. I am too close to my son, circumstances, emotions, and memories to receive in the same way that I received from Fara. Even now, I am limited in receiving for myself because I am subjective, and objectivity is required for mediumship. For the same reason, I am somewhat limited in what I can receive for other loved ones here, and from others I know in spirit.

I could not have received evidential validations from Perry. For example, I knew Perry was wearing black and white Vans with skinny jeans on the day of his passing. I knew he was wearing his favorite green t-shirt. I knew he was riding a bike. It was amazing to witness Perry having a conversation with someone here who he couldn't have known in body. He had an impact on someone here, connected with a stranger here. This is another beautiful aspect of mediumship.

My connection with Perry, through Fara, affirmed my trust in the connection I had and will always have with my son. This is one of the things I love most about serving others through mediumship. When I hear mediums tell others they can learn to connect and don't need a medium, I tend to assume the medium has not experienced the death of someone extremely close to them.

While this statement can be considered true, the dynamic of connecting with my son is much different than mediumship. For this reason, I carefully choose my words to others when I speak of mediumship and connecting with our own loved ones. I do not want to imply unrealistic expectations to those who already have enough grief to carry.

Our loved ones in spirit do frequently connect with us! You don't have to be a medium to experience this connection. Nor do you have to "learn" how to connect, because you are probably already experiencing connection! You only need to possess a realistic understanding of what connection with your loved one looks, sounds, and feels like.

Familiar thoughts come to mind which our loved ones impress upon us, yet we think we're recalling a memory or thinking of our loved one. We see a sign, but the next second we doubt and want someone else to validate our experience for us. We hear a quick hello and think it's our imagination. This is how subtle and natural our connections are, and how we are, most likely, overlooking our connections.

I passionately believe we all have a spiritual connection with those we love who have died. It's not predictable and loud and ongoing, but in subtle and quiet and unexpected ways we are connecting with our own loved ones.

I understand what we can expect from connection with our loved ones. I also understand that mediumship is a vessel of divine healing for others and as such, it is to serve others. These are important distinctions to understand.

I do receive gratification helping others discover their connection with Spirit. Since 2018, I have been leading discernment groups where Spirit uses me to help others grow in trust of their soul connection(s) and their innate intuitive abilities, which naturally results in discerning a stronger connection with their departed loved ones. Spirit has also led people to me who have their own mediumship abilities. It is a joy and honor to play even a small role in their journeys.

20

Release

Had I not explored the emotional depth of my grief, I couldn't have released the burden of my grief. While this was the human work I had to do, this was holy work, resulting in spiritual growth. Spirit took me to higher realms because I sat in lower realms. The heights I rose to were in proportion to the depths I sat in.

I had to see all the dirt and feel all the muck—my trauma, anger, guilt, shame, sorrow, and pain. I had to pull everything out of the emotional closet of my heart and live among the mess spread out in front of me. I had to sort through it all before I could let go.

Through the process of sorting, I kept so much good. The lessons mined from my dark, bottomless closet of grief resulted in more healing and growth than I could have imagined. The more my heart released, the more clearly I began to discern when my mind was stuck where it no longer needed to be.

I began to feel the tension between what my mind wanted to do—ruminate—and what my soul wanted to do—release. I knew this meant my heart was ready to let go, but I didn't know if my mind could. It was late November when I began to intuit that, just maybe, I could break free from this tension.

I wanted to release. I felt as if I had been carrying a 100-pound backpack around my heart unknowingly, when all at once I became aware of its heaviness. I began to buckle under its weight. In hindsight, I probably wasn't ready to let the weight go until this point, and my sudden awareness indicated I was ready.

My mind went to war with my soul and only one could direct my path. I distinctly remember several days of feeling myself wrapped up in this battle. My new awareness of this tension created angst within me, and that is exactly why I remember these days so succinctly.

I wanted to lay down the cross I was carrying, but I knew I needed God's help, so I asked.

It was my third day of experiencing this internal conflict when I visited a new church with my family. We arrived on a Sunday morning and walked Rayanna to the teen building. Jonas walked with us, but he wanted to attend the adult service with me and Craig.

Craig and I introduced ourselves to the adult youth leader at Rayanna's service. As we chatted, I noticed young men in the background who appeared to be Perry's age, walking around and goofing off. My tears stayed at bay as I focused on the conversation, smiling and replying appropriately with the youth leader.

I sighed in relief when the conversation ended, and we quietly walked back to the main building. We were walking in silence when Jonas, now twelve, said, "Mom, the past is the past." My heart had been longing for Perry, which then took me to the what-ifs, but I hadn't expressed this aloud. Jonas's unexpectedly profound statement abruptly brought me to the present moment.

The three of us found the main sanctuary and picked out seats. I mumbled along with the worship music before the pastor introduced himself and read announcements. He began his sermon with, "Leave the past in the past."

The pastor reached the end of his sermon when he shared a personal example from his own life. His story began with, "When our son was dying…" I had no idea he was a bereaved father.

A major shift occurred within me that Sunday, but I can't say I never questioned after that day. Mental patterns had become habitual, so they tended to come back. The difference was that, moving forward, I was able to observe my thoughts and redirect them. And remembrance of that Sunday gave me the determination to refocus when I needed to.

Unhealthy thoughts had become my default mode, but from that day forward they were never again my standard operating procedure. God always responds when we are willing to release and ask for help in doing so.

21

Heaven

Our first Thanksgiving was extremely difficult for me. I had days after Thanksgiving and leading up to Christmas that were excruciatingly painful. Overall, Christmas Day was softer than Thanksgiving had been, probably because my parents came from Tennessee to spend Christmas with us. Most painful for me was New Year's 2016. Longing for Perry took over in the days between Christmas and January 1. My heart was crushed with the thought of a year Perry wouldn't be a part of.

I forced myself out of the house on December 30 to go to the bank. On the drive I wept uncontrollably. I cried aloud to Perry, telling him how much I missed him and how hard it was to leave him behind in 2015. By the time I parked at the bank, I regained my composure. Just before I got out of my car, I heard Perry's voice in my head, "Don't leave!" and "behind."

I questioned if I had really heard Perry's voice because it had happened so quickly. I couldn't make sense of what he had communicated, if it had been Perry. I went into the bank and when I returned to the car, I started the engine before realizing my phone was not with me. I didn't think I'd taken my phone out of my purse in the bank, but I couldn't find it anywhere in the vehicle, so I retraced my steps back into the bank. I found my phone at the long prep counter where I had filled out my bank slips.

I almost left my phone behind. I now understood Perry's message! He really had been with me, but he had been more focused on the present moment than I had been. Spirit always is.

Shortly after my bank trip, Perry began appearing to me with other children, seemingly out of nowhere during my waking hours. I saw him in spirit image, in my left field of vision. My left side is also where I usually feel him. By "spirit image," I mean that I saw him in front of me, not as an image in my mind's eye or head. I didn't see Perry in front of me as a solid being, but he was real and moving and animated, communicating with me in the present moment, as if on a screen in front of me. This is how people in spirit visually project themselves to me.

I also see mental images from people in spirit in my mind, but this is more from a memory, not how a person in spirit would project themselves to me in the present moment. What I see in my mind are typically earthly images and scenes people in spirit may show me.

Visions began coming with greater depth. I was understanding more and gaining greater clarity. Life began to take on a surreal quality as my awareness of the greater reality expanded. Heaven really was living among us! I was excited and eager to share my experiences with others who would listen with an open mind.

Craig and our kids listened to my stories. It was all I could talk about, until I'd see their eyes glaze over. They were interested in my experiences, but only to a point. I liken this to when Craig explains something mechanical or technical to me.

Craig is very intelligent and extremely gifted in all things mechanical, but I can only comprehend so much when he attempts to explain such details to me. He will lose my attention, usually after a few minutes. This perspective helps me not to take it personally when others can't relate to me. I just think of my husband and the patience he has had with me over the years!

I have two separate memories that stand out around this time. Both times I was driving, and Perry appeared to me with a young man. Both times, Perry appeared to be buddy-buddy with each guy. I knew both of their parents, and I received quick words and validations for them. These were young men whom I knew Perry would have enjoyed hanging out with in life as well.

I came to learn that if I saw Perry next to another young person, they were close to the same age here on earth. My experience deepened when I saw Perry with younger children. Rather than simply appear with them, Perry took me to what looked like a place in heaven for young children.

This began happening with children of parents in bereaved support groups I was a part of. Perry would show up, interacting with the child of another parent. I saw other loved ones as well, not just bereaved children. I saw spouses and siblings and friends in spirit, embracing or sitting next to their loved ones here. Yet I only saw Perry with children close to his age or younger.

I knew something I hadn't previously known about my spiritual experiences. The connections were alive. These were back and forth conversations in the present moment. Spirit wasn't dropping visions into my mind for me to figure out later but engaging with me in mutual conversation. These were much different than human conversations, but my soul was an equal participant in these conversations, nonetheless.

I became aware that Spirit responded to my own thoughts after I received impressions. Spirit knew when I was confused and answered my questioning thoughts before I even understood Spirit knew my thoughts. Spirit also knew the thoughts of their loved ones here and answered their questions in the present moment, through me. Once I began serving Spirit and having three-way conversations, this aspect of communication became obvious to me.

As I began releasing the unknowns around Perry's death, Spirit began showing me specific and otherwise unknown details regarding others' deaths, to help their loved ones here receive answers or clarity. My heart gratefully accepted this ministry that I never could have seen coming.

I knew what grief experiences looked like, sounded like, and felt like. I have well-traveled roads paved of tragedy and mourning that Spirit can easily use to bring healing messages to their loved ones here. I never could have anticipated this would, or even could, happen!

In February I belonged to several online bereaved support groups. One group was for parents whose children had died by accidents of all types. I made a friend in this group, Teresa, whom I now know was Spirit-led to help me begin connecting with others. Later, Teresa would help arrange my first official session. It was in the group with Teresa that Perry introduced me to younger children in heaven. My earliest connections were made in this group and they were most instrumental to my learning and growth.

It was during this time that Perry introduced me to Jalissa. This connection was different in that Perry didn't simply appear before me. I saw Perry ahead of me, from behind, and I followed him through what looked like a beautiful park-like setting. I was wide awake, standing in my bedroom at the time, but I was in this daydream with Perry.

I felt as if Perry was showing me around. I looked around and saw young children happily playing, dancing, and creating art. A little girl who looked to be around five years old came up to Perry. She was smiling and seemed happy to see him, as if she was acquainted with Perry. She had dark hair that was pulled back, with a few loose tendrils, so I knew she had curly hair.

This little girl had the most loving smile and most joyful energy! Although Perry stood between us, I could see she wore a princess dress, and she began twirling around in it. Her dress was sparkly, and she wore white shoes.

This beautiful little princess took Perry's hand and led him to what looked like a buffet of ice cream and candy toppings. Perry stood in front of what appeared to be a soft serve ice cream machine. He seemed to be helping this little girl get ice cream, but then I saw her with a glass, and I could see that milkshakes were being dispensed from the machine.

The little girl began drinking a milkshake, and an immense smile spread across her face. I heard an L sound that I knew was in her name, and I saw the letter A. Then, I accidentally typed the letter J as I was messaging with her mother, Harmony, who had reached out to me after she had been given my information by Teresa.

I relayed the above impressions and more to Harmony. Harmony replied affirmatively about the letters in her daughter's name. Her daughter loved strawberry milkshakes, but she couldn't drink them here (on earth) because they upset her stomach.

Harmony's daughter was five years old when she passed. She loved princess dresses and dancing. Her body was buried in a sparkly dress and white shoes. As I shared more, Harmony replied, and then I was shown more from Perry and Harmony's daughter, Jalissa.

Jalissa showed me a little dog. Harmony told me she had adopted a Shih Tzu since Jalissa had passed. Jalissa showed me her big brother here and a marble of his she used to play with. She showed me what looked like a fort that she and her brother enjoyed playing in together. Jalissa shared with me that it was a tent.

Jalissa passed away in an auto accident, but she showed me that she swam up to a bright light, like a mermaid, when she (suddenly) left her body. I was shown a man in spirit who reached for sweet Jalissa's hand and, from heaven, pulled her up into his arms. I described this man as I saw him to Harmony, and she recognized him as her father, Jalissa's grandfather, who was in heaven, too.

The same day, Perry took me to another young girl, Amberly, who was also five years old when she passed. This sweet little girl had lighter, straight hair with blonde sun-streaked highlights. Amberly seemed to be more casual, rough-and-tumble, than Jalissa. She had a flushed and exhilarated look, as if she had just come in from playing outside, when I saw her sitting at a round kids' table.

Unlike Jalissa, who had walked up to Perry and taken his hand, Perry pulled up a chair and sat down beside Amberly. I saw that Perry was sitting in a kids' chair that was too small for him. I saw that Amberly was looking down, very focused and intent on what she was doing. I saw she was coloring with a blue crayon. Then I saw her paper and the house she was coloring on it.

I could see and feel other children playing happily around Amberly and Perry, yet Amberly was contentedly focused on coloring her blue house. Then, Amberly began talking to Perry as she was coloring, but I couldn't hear, feel, or know what was being said.

Flashes of images came to mind. I saw an outside scene, a horse, siblings, a red hat, a ring too small, and other images. I wasn't sure what these images meant, as they moved in and out of my view of Perry and Amberly at the coloring table.

Later the images would make sense to Serena, Amberly's mother, and I was shown more about a couple of these individual validations.

I sensed the next impressions in a way that was new for me. I began to feel a different environment around me. At the same time, I was fully aware of my physical surroundings. I was sitting in my bedroom, fully present in the moment, yet I was also experiencing another recent time and place on earth.

I was outside. I felt warm and humid air, as if it was summer or an unusually warm day. I saw green grass all around me and somehow, I was aware of physical surroundings I could not see. I was in a yard, near a house, and I knew there were other houses within view. Open land, more expansive than what is typical for a neighborhood or subdivision, surrounded me.

Then the scenery began moving. I felt and saw a woman's wet hair on her shoulders. I could see her neck and chest and the shirt she was wearing. I saw a road ahead of me, and this view of the road kept coming back to me. I felt and knew that all of this was around the time of Amberly's passing, so I thought maybe she passed from an accident on a road. I could assume it was an accident because of the support group her mother, Serena, was in. It was the road I had misunderstood.

Serena shared with me that Amberly passed as a result of an ATV accident on their property, not on the road. Serena had been running, carrying her little girl in her arms, to get her to the driveway, to the road, where she could be transported to the hospital. I understood what I previously hadn't . . . I had been experiencing the scene and memories from the perspective of Amberly as she was leaving her body. I saw the road because this is an image Amberly would have seen at this time, not because she passed on a road.

I didn't know what was happening at the time, but this was my first remote viewing experience. In a remote viewing experience, I see images or scenes from a last vivid memory, through another's eyes, so to speak. This is often when one leaves their body in a state of unconsciousness, which may be prior to when one's heart stops beating.

As we become unconscious to our earthly world, we become fully conscious of being surrounded by God's love and light, angels, and loved ones who have passed. Even with a sudden passing, I know this to be true, and I learned this first from Amberly.

My connection with Amberly was also the first time the same impressions kept coming back to me. This means something is not connecting, either with me or the receiver, yet Spirit wants it to be understood or remembered. This is Spirit's way of making a big deal out of something. If I don't understand I may never know, but when a receiver doesn't understand, there is a good chance they will remember or understand later, if Spirit and I make a big deal about it.

Throughout this connection I repeatedly saw Amberly coloring her blue house, so I repeatedly shared this with Serena, who didn't understand the significance in the moment. Amberly knew her persistence would ensure her mother would not forget. Months later, Serena messaged me to tell me it hit her why Amberly had been coloring a blue house: "Her burial vault was built like a doll house or playhouse, and it was painted blue."

I had another unique experience with sweet Amberly and her loving mother. The morning after our connection, I was at the vet with our dog, where a little girl was sitting in the waiting room with a Chihuahua. The little girl looked up at me and gave me the biggest smile. When she smiled, I felt a connection with Amberly, who hadn't previously been on my mind.

This unusual experience stayed with me, so later I messaged Serena. I asked her if she happened to have a Chihuahua. They had a Chihuahua who had passed away earlier in the same summer Amberly passed away, Serena told me. No doubt, Amberly wanted her mom to know they are together.

My connection with Amberly and Serena is a reminder to me that the connections which have taught me the most are the ones that totally confused me, where I may have bombed the delivery! When new information of any kind is first thrown at us, we don't know what to make of it. It takes time and experience with the information to assimilate, to learn. Fluency with our Spirit language requires immersion, and this was a full immersion lesson for me!

Thankfully, even though I was overwhelmed by these new sensory experiences and had difficulty interpreting and relaying, Serena still trusted me. She was reassuring and encouraging and gracious to me. Spirit had divinely orchestrated this connection between Amberly and her mom to benefit me as well as Serena. I am grateful to Serena and sweet Amberly for the amazing teachers they were to me.

Teresa had connected me with these parents. Right away, she seemed to know who to send to me. I quickly discerned her selflessness and compassion by the way she genuinely wanted to help other parents.

It wasn't until after I connected with the other parents that I connected with Teresa's own daughter in spirit, Jo, while I was sitting in a parking lot after I had dropped my daughter off for a class. I first saw Perry and a feisty, active, and red-haired young lady beside him. My focus was on Perry as I waited for what was becoming familiar to me—a spiritual introduction.

Perry was quiet for this connection, though. The young lady was more animated. I began to connect more with Jo than Perry, feeling her personality and spirit. She turned to Perry and said, "I've got this, dude!" Jo took over, which gave Teresa and I both a chuckle. Teresa replied, "That would be her!"

Jo was twenty-five when she passed. After our session, I connected the dots. Perry had never introduced me to anyone more than a couple years older than him. But after this meeting, even younger children began to show up on their own, without Perry's presence, or at least without his presence being obvious to me. The timing fascinated me. Everything had been divinely orchestrated.

This was representative of my spiritual growth, but it also represented where I was in my healing, as a bereaved mother. Outside of my connections around this time, I began to feel more secure in my ongoing relationship with Perry, even when I didn't see him or feel him, and even when I didn't notice signs from him.

My emotions started leveling out, rather than going up with signs of Perry's presence and down when I wasn't getting signs or feeling him. It was a bit sad to no longer see Perry in each connection, but it was a sign of my healing. I believe Perry's quiet exit from my connections aligned with my confidence in Spirit. More importantly, his exit aligned with me coming to emotional acceptance of his death.

Perry didn't permanently exit. At times he helped me behind the scenes, which is what he would have preferred here! I must thank Jo who, no doubt, helped behind the scenes as well, before and after that evening.

I continued to see Perry from time to time. He showed up to demonstrate something new or give me extra help. To this day, Perry can and does show up to help me out, and I'm certain he helps me out even when I am unaware he is around. Occasionally, another person in spirit will refer to Perry, more so around meaningful days for our family, his birthday, and the annual marking of his passing.

After Jo's, "I've got this dude," a mother reached out to me. Like most of my connections at the time, we connected via text. I was sitting in my bed when I felt this mother's daughter. Then, she appeared as a beautiful young woman, floating above me. There seemed to be significance around me being in bed, as if this young lady wanted me to know that she knew I was in bed. She was wearing a beautiful white flowy gown or dress, and she was exquisitely beautiful.

I didn't know what to make of it all, but I relayed my impressions to her mother. This connection was unique in that the mother told me her daughter had visited her in a dream, appearing the way I had described from my vision. I understood why her daughter had been focusing on me being in bed! This was my first experience of receiving impressions of a dream visit.

Parents continued to reach out to me as they heard of me through others. Sometimes visions, feelings, words, and/or thoughts would come to me in a moment, while I read an email or text. Other times, impressions came later. Either way, most parents were willing to share with me what the significance was or wasn't. Above all, I appreciated their willingness to share with me what was incorrect because this helped me learn and grow more than I otherwise could have.

As my trust in Spirit grew, I learned what comes to me from Spirit is one hundred percent accurate, but my human interpretation and translation is less accurate. I'm the middleman and as such, the messages I share come through my human filter, logical reasoning, and frames of reference. I take great care to be as objective as possible; however, I'm still human.

It wasn't my genius, but my willingness to admit and see when and where I was wrong, that allowed for growth. I really had to overcome self-consciousness and not be hard on myself when I was wrong. With experience, I got better at staying in a place of objective curiosity rather than shrinking down into my ego when I didn't understand what something meant or got a "no."

I tried not to make assumptions that an impression always has the same meaning. I paid attention to context and began to discern subtle and more complex nuances in communication with Spirit.

This growth required that I remained in a state of learning from my inaccuracies. It took time and lots of practice, but I came to enjoy learning from my mistakes as much as I enjoyed the wondrous validations that came through. The validations are from Spirit and never to my credit, anyway. All I can give myself credit for is my ability to get out of my own way.

I am most grateful for the beautiful souls here who were willing to help me learn and grow by sharing more with me, especially when I messed up. Spirit knew my connections with other bereaved folks would be my perfect training ground, serving the highest good of all, myself included.

On another day in February, I was talking to Jonas in his room when I saw a young man in spirit. He said he liked the cards Jonas was playing with. It took me a minute but then I connected who he was—Arthur. His mom, Sarah, was a friend I had made in Tom Zuba's group.

Arthur brought through other validations for his mom while we texted. We connected again down the road, and while on my way home prior to our session, Jonas made a joke, and I heard Arthur laugh and say, "I like him, he's funny!"

It was new and unusual for someone in spirit, unknown to me here in this lifetime, to interact with me in such a personal, fun way and include my family in the interaction! It's intriguing to me that Arthur's mom and I were and are friends, and Arthur was so friendly with me and my son.

There is another synchronicity in that Jonas is Perry's younger brother… Arthur's younger brother Max joined him in heaven fifteen months after Arthur passed. These tight-knit brothers both passed from melanoma, and they were able to experience their cancer journey here at the same time. One thing extraordinary about their lives and deaths is that Arthur and Max were born fifteen months apart and they died fifteen months apart, both at 24 years old.

I have since met Max in spirit. He and Arthur share such a powerful brotherly bond that when they have come to me, my challenge has been figuring out who is saying what! Like other things, I have learned to accept I may not figure it out perfectly, but Mom always understands. Mom knows best, that is for sure!

22

Jesus and Me

The first few months of 2016 felt like a launch in a Spirit rocket with no time to question what was happening. Spirit was teaching me so much in a short window of time. After each connection, I was left scratching my head at new aspects I didn't understand. I came to understand this was good—a sign that Spirit was continuously teaching me more.

By the end of March, I began to yearn for routine and consistency in my life. Emotionally, I felt like I had been in grief intensive care and now I was antsy to enter the step-down unit. I wanted to begin fully participating in life again, but it would be a long time before I could consistently do so. I was seeing the spirit world in color, but I longed to see my world in color again.

Connecting with other bereaved parents brought me comfort, and my connections with Spirit were extraordinarily healing and wondrous experiences. Still, I had learned that doing my part for my own healing was something I needed to prioritize. I still needed grief support, but I needed life support, too.

I began attending more fitness classes and making an effort to meet new people. I picked up responsibilities Craig and I had shelved when Perry died. Clutter had accumulated that needed to be dealt with. Meal planning needed to be picked back up. Grocery shopping had consisted of what was convenient or tasty, and I had thirty pounds to show for it.

I felt relieved and grateful for this new motivation, yet I felt overwhelmed and lost and ill-equipped to move out of survival mode. I experienced new moments of passion to begin life anew, yet I experienced frustration when the moments didn't last.

At this point in my spiritual journey, I was aware I had the ability mediums were known to possess—communication with the other side. It would be months before I would be brave enough to call myself a medium, but I wondered if I could schedule connections, because I craved structure that unplanned connections were not providing for me.

I felt apprehensive for multiple reasons, so I asked God to guide me and help me discern which feelings to follow.

I began to pray for direction. It was around this time that I also found a Christian mentorship group for people with psychic and mediumship gifts, led by a selfless woman who is an extremely gifted medium. She gave her own time and energy to help me understand my gifts. Although the group was in my life for a short season, I will forever be grateful for Elizabeth Vida-Granrath's wise counsel and guidance.

Scripture that had previously been mysterious and confusing to me now made sense, viewed through my new lens of greater awareness. I searched the scriptures to understand more about the stigma of using the term medium to describe my abilities. I wasn't sure what mediums in the Bible did, but my research proved to me it had nothing to do with what I (or most modern mediums) do.

I couldn't even fathom being associated with child sacrifice. I knew biblical references didn't relate to those who connect through God's love. I could and did allow biblical comparison to offend me, but now I don't.

I do not consider myself a medium in the biblical sense of the term, but I do have the spiritual gift of discerning spirits. I prayed about using the term prophet in my work, but to me, the term implies more psychic and intuitive abilities. I could foresee how calling myself a prophet might result in many awkward and confusing conversations.

I have prophetic gifts, but Spirit had made my spiritual strengths obvious to me. I connect loved ones living on opposite sides of the veil. My spiritual gift is to help grieving people heal and I needed to be honest and authentic in presenting myself.

I would be lying to say I was comfortable using the term medium. I have met many mediums since beginning my journey, and I have been pleasantly surprised to learn I was not alone in my discomfort. Many mediums use false names or remain in the medium closet for this very reason. I don't judge them for it, but I wasn't going to do that.

While sitting on my patio one morning in prayer about this, I felt enveloped by the presence of Christ and heard, "It matters not. Do my work. Let others stay in judgment." This gave me all the confidence I needed and would ever need to confidently serve Spirit.

This was a season I felt very close to Christ. I was coming out of the medium closet and being true to who I had been created to be. As I began to step more fully into who I inherently was and am, I experienced judgment, usually masked behind cordial words of pity, with scriptural references attached to them.

I don't know whose god would allow a grief-stricken bereaved mother to be deceived by the devil, but not my God. My body, mind, and heart may have been weak, but my spirit had never been stronger, nor had I ever felt more closely connected to God.

I arranged my first scheduled session through my friend Teresa, Jo's mom. I felt impressed to connect with someone I couldn't possibly know. Teresa passed my information along to someone she knew and per my request, Teresa informed the person I wanted their anonymity to be preserved. Teresa let her acquaintance know it was my first time scheduling a session and I wasn't sure if it would work. That took some of the pressure off.

My first official client reached out to me via email without any other identifying information. Then my nerves kicked in. *If I schedule a session myself, will the holy spirit still be leading?* I wasn't certain I would receive anything.

Fears came to the surface. *If I didn't allow it to just happen randomly, would I be controlling the connection? And if I was controlling the connection, by doing so, would I be inviting unwelcome spirits to me?* I had never communicated with negative or evil energies, entities, or spirits, and I certainly didn't want to! *Would I be conjuring?*

Aside from my first question, I intuited the other thoughts were fear-based, and my fears had never served my highest good. I only connected through God's love, so I knew one of two things would happen. My first appointment would go well, or nothing would happen.

I arranged to connect via phone with my first client on the following Sunday evening. By Friday, I knew Spirit was leading my steps. That was when I had a serious talk with Jesus. I asked him to give me obvious and clear validation, either way. I was willing to serve in this new way, even if it meant making others uncomfortable. I was equally willing to take a blow to my ego if it meant staying in God's will.

On Saturday morning, I woke up to my friend's adult son in spirit, Matty, hovering above me. Matty's mother, Diane, and I had met in Tom Zuba's "Living WITH the Holidays" program. We became fast and close friends. When I saw

Matty Saturday morning, he was glowing radiantly, smiling his big, open Matty smile. I felt his big, warm signature Matty hug.

By this point, I felt as if I had come to know Matty through Diane's stories and through connecting with him. After Matty showed up, I anticipated a message for Diane, because that is typically how things go. This time I didn't receive anything else from Matty. This left me in a state of anticipatory curiosity.

I planned to share with Diane, but first I needed to eat breakfast. As I was preparing breakfast, Diane came to mind and I discerned Spirit had brought her to mind. I texted Diane and figured Matty would give me more while we were texting, but that didn't happen.

Diane did share with me about an upcoming road trip with her sister. When I read the word "sister" I got goosebumps, my Spirit signal to pay attention. I was even more curious, and I wondered if more was yet to come.

On Sunday afternoon, I went to the mall with my family. While walking with Craig, my right knee unexpectedly went out. I lost feeling in my knee. There was no logical explanation, and this had never happened to me before. I wondered if it was a Spirit thing, if this would somehow connect with my first client? After I spoke these thoughts aloud to Craig, the feeling in my knee came back. I continued walking as normal.

While at the mall, I read about "clairsentience" (feeling in an intuitive or spiritual sense) in a book. After I returned home from the mall, I called Diane to share what I had learned. She gave me an example of knee pain, and I hadn't even told Diane about my knee going out at the mall. Diane was a friend who enjoyed hearing about my spiritual experiences. I loved sharing with Diane because she possessed more knowledge of spiritual matters than I did.

We were both newly bereaved with sons in heaven. We were both passionate about the topic of Spirit communication. I was learning at lightning speed, and it was welcoming to have a friend who shared in my excitement. I appreciated learning from Diane as much as she appreciated hearing my stories.

When my client called me Sunday evening, I immediately heard "sister" in my mind. It turned out my client wanted to connect with her sister-in-law, who is like a sister to her. My first official session was the most extensive connection I had ever experienced.

The session began with feeling as if I had been placed in a back bedroom where my client's sister-in-spirit had passed. I was shown a moving view of the room, and the view stopped at an empty chair. I instantly knew this meant someone wanted to be there who couldn't be there. I saw details around the room, and I saw when my client's sister-in-spirit left her body.

The sweet sister-in-spirit communicated being grateful that she was cared for at home by her family. She was grateful that they kept her pain controlled. She expressed loving validations about her husband and showed me how she had been with him since she passed. She showed me a collection of coins sitting on her gravesite and a memorable quilt, among other significant validations.

Every validation held meaning for my client. At the end of our time together, the sister-in-spirit showed me that she was present in spirit at a race, waving a flag. My client told me she had picked up running after her sister-in-spirit passed, and she had run her first race on this very morning. Her sister-in-spirit had been at her race, cheering her along!

I thanked my client and then I thought to ask her if she happened to have any knee issues. She told me while she was running that morning, her right knee gave out. She was planning to go to the doctor the next morning.

I'm not sure I've ever had a connection that was so clear and easy for me to figure out! I must admit, I was a little disappointed to learn that not all connections would continue to be so easy or clear! I was blown away that Spirit could give me so much information at once, and I could understand it all. The experience was massive validation from Spirit that I was on the right path for me.

There was no room for doubt. I was on cloud nine for quite a while after that first official session. When I went to bed Sunday night, I told Craig, "Jesus gave me his blessing, and he sent me Matty and Diane."

23

New Horizons

That first planned session gave me the confidence I needed, not only to continue in my new work, but to live confidently and honestly about who I was, free from fear of what others might think or say. Clients reached out to me after hearing about me via word of mouth. I worked for several months at no charge, connecting with four or five people a week, via text or phone.

After several months I began accepting donations. I was at a place financially where I would have otherwise needed to work again. What I earned from donations paid for our extra family expenses that Craig's income did not cover. I am grateful that Craig was (and still is) extremely supportive, and we were content that Spirit met our needs.

I was pleasantly surprised by the generosity of clients. I didn't yet have an established reputation. I could have spent time, energy, and money marketing paid services, but instead I spent time and energy honing my abilities, bringing healing to others almost every day. Word of mouth was and still is my marketing. Everything was a win-win-win situation those early months of working in my new vocation.

By May 2016, I was absolutely in love with serving Spirit and bringing healing to other bereaved folks here. Connections were going well, but May was otherwise a very difficult month for me. May ushered in Perry's birthday, Mother's Day, and what would have been Perry's graduation from high school.

There were a couple things we did that made May much more bearable. In March, we began a stuffed animal drive for Sailor Kate Ministry. Shortly after Perry passed, one of the messages I intuited from God was to channel my love for Perry into others. Of course, this had more meaning than I could have known at the time!

Sailor Kate Ministry is named after a sweet baby girl in heaven, Sailor Kate. Sailor Kate Ministry sent stuffed animals to Rayanna and Jonas after Perry died. I wanted to channel my love for Perry into others for his birthday, and I appreciated that Sailor Kate had reached out to our family.

It felt good to shop, deliver, and send stuffed love to bereaved and sick children. Our Sailor Kate drive filled some of my emptiness from not having Perry's party to plan or gifts to buy for him. My mom flew in the week before Perry's birthday. Along with me and the kids, she helped us shop and mail stuffed animals out to children all over the US and other countries.

We delivered stuffed animals to local bereaved siblings, daughters, and sons. Our kids took extra stuffed animals to our local fire station. We didn't do this alone. Many people sent stuffed animals to us in advance. The generosity of others filled our hearts and our home as we watched our dining room fill up with fun and colorful stuffed animals of all shapes and sizes.

As a family, we went on a three-day cruise for Perry's birthday, May 8. My mom went with us. We received amazing signs the day of his birthday as we drove to southern California. At the end of the cruise while we were waiting to disembark, I felt Spirit around me. We were in a crowd of people, so I was confused. I don't reach out to strangers with impressions, and everyone aboard was a stranger to me, so Spirit had taken me by complete surprise.

We experienced a delay in disembarking. I prayed that if there was something I was supposed to do, Spirit would make it obvious to me. Then I felt drawn to a man to my right. I prayed Spirit would arrange for our paths to cross if I was supposed to say something to him.

A few minutes later my eye caught the patio where this same man stood by himself. He had previously been surrounded by his family, within the crowd of people gathered in the dining room, waiting to disembark. As I pondered if this was a sign, I felt Spirit's presence intensify, which for me means yes.

I walked out onto the deck and tried to look natural. I was nervous because I hadn't yet received any impressions to share. I leaned on the rail, standing an acceptable distance from the man, when he looked at me. His gaze held mine. I still hadn't received more from Spirit, so I smiled and before I could talk myself out of it, I nervously asked, "Would you have happened to lose someone recently?"

The man looked silently at me for what seemed like a very long time. It was only a few seconds. I still hadn't received anything else from Spirit. The man asked me if I was "of God?" *Um, yes!* His reply took me off guard. "Oh, yes," I answered. He proceeded to share with me how his nephew had died just before the cruise.

The cruise had been a family reunion for their entire family and despite their sorrow, the man's family knew his nephew would want them to keep their plans. The man's adult nephew had been swimming with his children when his nephew's son began to drown. His nephew died saving his own son from drowning. I expressed my condolences and the man replied, "I know God sent you to me. Thank you."

This surprise meeting reinforced what Spirit began teaching me before Perry died—Spirit will arrange meetings if there is a strong need. I was nervous on the cruise ship because I hadn't received any impressions, but this man wouldn't have been comfortable with more. Spirit knew that. I only needed to follow Spirit's lead.

We made it through May. One day in June, the kids and I visited a local waterpark. I had fun all day, and the kids were still going strong as the sun began to set. Dusk no longer gave me anxiety, but I still felt a heaviness when the sun set, especially when I was tired.

We ate dinner at the waterpark. Then Rayanna wanted to go off in one direction with her friend, who had come with us, while Jonas wanted to hit up the wave pool. I would be able to see him and there were many lifeguards. Safety wasn't an issue, but I knew Jonas preferred company, and he didn't have accompanying friends. I had enjoyed the waterpark with him, but now I needed a break.

Perry should be here with Jonas. I thought of how unfair our situation was. Tears flooded my eyes. Perry would have been so much more fun than me! Perry loved Jonas and being his big brother, and there was no one Jonas adored more than Perry. I encouraged Jonas to go ahead without me. I would join him after a few minutes of rest, I told him.

I sat down on a lounge chair and imagined Perry jumping in the wave pool with Jonas, encouraging him to go deeper and jump higher. My heart hurt and hot tears streamed down my face. I began talking to Perry in my mind and under my breath. I cried while telling him how much I missed him and how hard this all was. I gazed toward the sunset, breathing in the sky's beauty as an attempt to soften the moment for me.

Unexpectedly, I heard Perry's voice loud and clear and fast, "He'll make a friend, Mom!" I froze waiting for more, but that was all I heard. I looked toward Jonas where he was jumping in the waves. There were kids beside him, behind him, and in front of him, but he wasn't interacting with anyone. After he exited the wave pool, Jonas came up to me and with a smile, he said, "Mom, I made a friend!"

Shortly after our waterpark visit, I had a client no-show (one of the downsides to free and donation sessions). Craig was sitting in the adjoining room while I was waiting for my client to call.

I opened the door between us and said to Craig, "Too bad I can't connect for you." As I previously mentioned, it's difficult for me to receive from and for my own loved ones, yet I felt Spirit and began to wonder if I could connect for Craig. Maybe one of his grandparents . . .

I began to experience remote viewing. I was in a memory as a passenger riding in the front seat of a car. I saw that Craig was driving. I could hear laughter about an animal crossing the road in front of the car. I didn't feel any sense of personal familiarity with this memory.

Next, I was in an older home I didn't recognize. I was in a basement, and there was a pool table. Others were in the background and I was playing pool. I saw the carpet was a brightly colored shag, as if from the '70s. Nothing was familiar to me, but Craig understood it all to be connected to his great aunt's home in Nebraska.

Perry and Craig had taken a trip by themselves to Craig's grandmother's homestead in Nebraska for the burial of her ashes. I was seeing the scenes from Perry's memory of it. Craig and Perry had played pool together in the basement of Craig's great aunt's home, Craig told me.

Needless to say, this was a fascinating experience for me. I saw scenes, but somehow my own emotions never engaged. I felt very objective, as I do when I connect for others. I'm sure Spirit protected my own emotions from engaging so that I wouldn't lose my connection.

This is the only mediumship connection I have experienced with Perry, and it could only have happened with a memory I hadn't experienced here. I had never visited the home or town from this memory Perry shared with me. I hadn't met the people I saw in Perry's memory, aside from Craig and Perry. My unfamiliarity is what caused me to be an objective and pure vessel, helping Perry share a memory with his dad.

24

Special Connections

It is impossible for me to share all the memorable, fascinating, and healing connections I have experienced with others since beginning my spiritual work. I hope to include more in a future book, but for now I want to share just a few extra special connections that hold personal significance to me. These are connections that have taken place since the year following Perry's death.

In February 2017, a most beautiful red-haired young lady in spirit introduced herself to me. She appeared to me twice, and she showed up in two separate client sessions, all within a week's time. When she showed up in my clients' sessions, my clients could not identify her.

The young lady appeared to be in her early twenties, and she had the biggest, brightest smile. She wore different outfits each time I saw her. She was glowing, in radiant white light, and I could feel how very much at peace she was.

I was perplexed because I did not know who the young lady was connected to, but she knew exactly what she was doing.

At this same time, I was co-leading a Facebook-based support group for bereaved parents. A week after my mysterious new friend appeared to me, a new member of the group, Misty, introduced herself to the group on the Facebook page. Misty attached several photos of her beautiful red-haired daughter, Brianna, who had passed away just five weeks prior.

I immediately recognized Brianna as the young lady who had been making her presence known to me! I recognized two of the dresses Brianna wore in Misty's attached photos, because Brianna had been wearing the dresses two of the times she had appeared to me. This was the first and only time I have ever reached out to someone first online, but I had to.

I asked Misty if I could private message her, and she gave me permission to do so. I thought what I had to share would not be considered evidential to Misty, but I knew it had to be divinely timed. Misty's reply blew me away.

Misty told me a week earlier she had been on my website and read about Perry. Misty has given me permission to share her own words here:

"I looked up your page a week before I posted Bree's pics. That's when I told Bree, 'Baby, if this lady is for real, please go find Perry and tell him I need his mom to get a hold of me. Please Baby, find Perry!!' A week later you wrote on Brianna's pics and I was amazed . . . I was sitting outside holding my phone in my hand, because you were PMing me, and I looked up and said, 'Oh my God, Baby, he did it!!' And that was when I saw that big rainbow orb in the sky!! And you called!!"

In late July 2017, I met a young man in spirit via a letter from heaven. This is a connection where I don't have a receiver with me while I'm connecting. I connect with the receiver's loved one(s) in spirit, write down everything I receive, then email my impressions to my client.

When I worked my first letter from heaven, I was extremely

nervous! It was an experience of blind faith and trust. Without the "yes" or "no" from a receiver to help me know if I was on the right track, I wasn't always certain. Staring at the page of impressions and then hitting that send button was a courageous act, but the client replies made it worth it.

I have grown a lot through letters because there is a sense of clarity, and less distraction, when it is just me and Spirit. People often ask me about this, how connection works if they are not present when I connect with their loved ones. The answer is quite simple. It's only their intention that matters, not time. Heaven doesn't experience linear and sequential time.

Letters work because a loved one here has set the intention to connect with a loved one in heaven. I connect through the eternal love and bond two souls share, yet these times of communication between me and Spirit have been very enlightening and sweet.

In this particular letter from heaven, the young man in spirit held up what looked like a license, but it wasn't a typical driver's license. I wondered if it was an exclusive driver's license or some other unique type of license. He was smiling and I felt a lot of pride from him. I noticed a sizable A on the license, with the color red around it.

These impressions came through strongly, but they did not connect with the recipient. I was confused but let it go, content that the other impressions connected and hopeful the license validation would soon make sense for the recipient.

A few days after the letter, on the second anniversary of Perry's death, July 27, 2017, Rayanna went on a campus tour of Arizona State University (ASU), the college she wanted to attend. We thought she would have to tour later, so this was a pleasant surprise for her.

During the campus tour that afternoon while we were in one of the common areas, the tour guide began talking about how the student ID also serves as an ATM card. The guide held up her ASU ID to demonstrate. There was a sizable A in the corner, with the color red around it.

The young man in spirit had been helping Perry congratulate and celebrate his sister on this day!

In September 2017, I connected with Carolyn and her grandson Matthew in spirit. I felt an immediate bond with Carolyn the moment I met her on the phone, and Matthew reminded me of Perry. Carolyn has since become a dear friend, and she is one of the most loving souls I have ever met.

Near the end of our session together, Matthew told me he was with Perry and they were having a fun time. This amused both me and Carolyn. I felt Matthew's humor and he said, "Perry's gonna make the dog bark at two in the morning!"

We do have a little dog, Finn, but he was (and is) an exceptional sleeper . . . and this was supposed to be Carolyn's gift, so I didn't know what to make of it all.

Finn goes to bed with us no matter how early, he stays in bed with us, and he sleeps in with us no matter how late. But that very night, following my time spent with Carolyn and Matthew, Craig and I woke up to Finn barking. Finn wasn't even on the bed with us, but standing between our bedroom and master bath, as if watching someone. I picked up my phone. It was exactly 2:00 a.m.

In April 2018, I connected with a young woman, Anna, and her father, Jim, in spirit. About halfway through our session, Jim showed me a realtor sign connected to someone here. I asked Anna about the realtor her father knows, but this did not connect with Anna. Jim continued to show me various impressions, but I related to them as real estate signs and symbols. Anna could not relate to any of these impressions.

I became increasingly confused. Everything had been flowing well up to this point, but the unplaced real estate impressions seemed to bring communication to a halt. I apologized to Anna and offered her another session soon, at no additional charge to her.

When I ended my session with Anna, I saw missed call notifications from our realtor on my phone. At this time, our house in Tennessee was under contract for sale, and we had placed an offer on a home in Arizona. Our Tennessee realtor had sent an email we hadn't received, and we needed to sign a significant document ASAP. Craig had been tied up in meetings at work, so neither of us had known about this.

Anna's father had been helping me! When I shared with Anna what happened, she told me that would be so typical of her dad to want to help me in that way. Anna shared with me that her father attended open houses just for fun, and he enjoyed helping his friends make deals.

I loved how Anna was open to this, and I loved how her father, Jim, brought fatherly guidance to me that day!

Another memorable fatherly connection was with a husband in spirit and his wife here. He was also a father, and he passed around the same age as Anna's father. When I first met him, I saw and felt him apply something wet to the tip of my nose, like a dot of lotion or paint.

It turned out this gentleman passed from skin cancer and I have a freckle on the tip of my nose. He had put sunscreen on the tip of my nose! I knew Spirit has no human eyes, nor did this gentleman carry a physical memory of me. Did Perry share about my freckle with him, behind the scenes? Possibly. When I put sunscreen on my nose, I often say hello to this gentleman and thank him for the reminder.

25

My Angel

I must share one more very significant connection. During the second year of my spiritual work I began to see a radiant, glowing feminine presence. I saw her in the same perspective I see departed loved ones—above and in front of me, as if from a projection of my mind's eye.

Even though I refer to my angel as a female, she has never presented herself to me in human form, nor has she ever shared any earthly memories with me. Although she appears to have a feminine face, I cannot discern specific facial features, nor do I feel specific personality traits from this divine being. In place of a body, I see billowy, radiant, white light.

What I feel from my angel is a maternal and unconditionally loving presence. She imparts upon me a strong sense of love for myself when she connects with me. I don't receive human references from my angel, but she can use earthly symbols I recognize to communicate messages to me. The symbols I receive from my angel are more consistent than what I might receive from an individual personality in spirit, although both experiences are akin to Spirit playing charades with me. The symbols my angel uses to communicate with me are more easily and clearly understood by me.

It is not obvious to me that my angel interacts with the

people in spirit I connect with, but I can tell she is aware of my spiritual work. She can guide me in preserving my energy for my work, but she is just as interested in other work I do and even my personal activities, as they align with my highest good. My angel may show up prior to a client session or even during a session, but her presence indicates a message for me, personally.

My angel's presence regarding my spiritual work gives me confidence and lets me know that everything is going to be okay. For this reason, it is not uncommon for me to see her prior to something unusual or distracting that occurs during a session.

When I first began to see my angel, what followed would be flashes of earthly images in my mind's eye that would have relevance later in my day. These future impressions were not related to my spiritual work. Even though I didn't understand this new spiritual presence in my life, my angel's quick and validating messages proved to me she was here to help me, and she seemed to have my best interest as her own. By the nature of her messages, I believe she knows everything about me, in all aspects of my life.

As an example, my angel may show up and hold up a stop sign while I am thinking about my plans for this evening, if the plans are not for my highest good. It's important I express that this doesn't need to be for a significant reason. I may not be avoiding a car accident by staying home, for example. I may simply be avoiding someone with negative energy or a situation that drains me if I choose to stay home for the evening.

My angel may also give me encouragement to try or do something I may not otherwise try or do. This does not mean I always make perfect decisions now, nor does my angel always step in or show up. I don't claim to know the rhyme or reason as to why she shows up in one situation over another, but I have learned to pay attention to my angel's presence in my life. My angel wants to help me not just with the big things or the spiritual things, but with all the things.

After only a few times of connecting with my angel, I was fairly certain she was indeed an angelic being and not someone who had lived an earthly life. If I was wrong, then I figured it just wasn't for my highest good to know any different. I did question if this wise and guiding feminine presence could have been a projection of my higher self, because of how she seemed to know everything about me.

Months after I first met my angel, I was soaking in the tub one evening when I had a powerful spiritual encounter I will never forget. I saw a radiant vision of Christ as he appeared in front of me. His presence was powerful yet loving. Christ's arms opened in front of me, and then I saw this same angel who had been appearing to me. She was positioned slightly below Christ, seemingly closer to me, as if Christ was presenting her to me. Then I saw Perry, slightly below her and to my left.

In this divine moment, I sensed the relationship between the three of them as being intimate and loving, and I felt as if they had been coming to me this way all along. They were all encompassed by bright white light, together.

This scripture came to mind:

He will put his angels in charge of you to protect you in all your ways.

Psalm 91:11

Yes! This is exactly what my angel had been doing and continues to do today. Through my angel's guidance, I have learned how to protect my energy, how and when to say no to things and people that are not in alignment with my highest good, and how to better love and care for myself.

I don't see my angel as much these days, but I suspect it is because she has taught me well. Many of the messages she used to give me I now receive through my intuition. I may still see her from time to time. She has helped me release. She has given me permission, or a heads up, to rest. She has brought me guidance regarding decisions I have struggled trusting my intuition about. Time and experience have validated that the guidance I receive from my angel is accurate and for my highest good.

Just as Perry gave me the trust and confidence I needed for my spiritual work, my angel lady has given me the trust and confidence I needed to serve my highest good.

I used to think that energy protection was all about protecting myself from dark or evil spirits in other realms. I've come to learn that protecting my energy is more about protecting myself from the negative people and circumstances that do not serve my highest good and might otherwise bring my energy down. I have my angel lady to thank for my new understanding of this.

I'd never felt the need to refer to my angel with a name, aware that this is a human desire. During times of contact with her, my spirit expresses acknowledgment and gratitude. When I'd share about my experiences with her to others, I was content to affectionately refer to her as "my angel lady."

A few months after my experience with Christ, my angel lady, and Perry, my angel appeared to me as I was drifting off to sleep. She said the name "Christa." My logical nature questioned, even in my dream state. I didn't know if she had said "Chrissa" or "Christa."

This was and is the only time I had ever heard my angel speak to me, and it was odd to me that she spoke such a normal and modern name. I woke up and googled the meaning of both names. The name Chrissa is a derivative of Christa, and the name Christa means follower of Christ.

Shortly after receiving my angel's name, I began to see other people's angels and the same symbolic language I recognized from my own angel, to share guidance with others. Our angels always surround us with support, and they only bring us loving guidance. We only need to ask.

I hope these special connections have proved to you that we need never doubt the expanse of loving, unseen support we have, in all areas of our lives. Spirit is behind us, beside us, and always leading our way.

26

Lessons from Grief

I am writing four years after my son's death. Within many chapters, I have shared some of my deeper insights and lessons learned from my experiences. It's important for me to express that I didn't come to these realizations at the time I was going through the experiences. Time, contemplation, and reflection have connected dots. I want to share additional lessons I have learned since Perry's death.

Before Perry died, I believed life wasn't fair. Perry's death didn't teach me this. We had friends—kind, loving parents—who experienced the death of their children. I cried with them, ached for them. Before Perry died, I absolutely believed we are not promised tomorrow, nor can we control the future.

There is a difference between believing and knowing. Death came to me personally, and now I have my own intimate reference point. The unimaginable is no longer a concept, but a reality. My perspective shifted from believing to knowing, and it was the knowing that allowed me to fully integrate belief into my life.

Knowing has gifted me the freedom to live as if I don't have complete control. I worry less and love more. I live more in the present moment. The bonus gift from living in the present moment is this: Worry cannot survive here. Additional gifts: The present moment is where there is no death, and our love is always alive.

Grief itself has grown me. Going through the most terrifying pain taught me not to fear pain. Maybe this is akin to parachuting out of a plane and overcoming a fear of heights, except that I didn't want my experience. Yet overcoming my fear of emotional pain has been another gift from my grief.

It would take a couple years following Perry's death for me to become comfortable with pain. At first, I was terrified of my grief. My pain was too intense and too consistently present for me to respect it for what is was—an indication I was releasing and healing.

Pain doesn't show up when it's convenient for me, but I give it my full attention, knowing it will leave and take with it that which no longer serves me. Pain has been my prelude to a next level of healing. Understanding pain has helped me focus on its result—more peace, love, and joy. I've come to view confronting my pain as delayed gratification, emotionally speaking.

Once my grief began to soften and take the backseat in my life, other painful experiences from my past resurfaced—hurts I thought I had healed from long ago. This was confusing for me because these offenses didn't compare to the devastation of losing my son. I didn't understand why I was finally getting back on my feet again, only to have past hurts come to mind in such a strong way.

Because Perry's death had taught me not to fear pain, the experience had paved a clear way for other unresolved pain to reveal itself, and then leave. That's all pain ever wants to do, I have learned.

Another lesson Perry's death taught me: There is no single or perfect way to mourn or to find healing. I did the best

I could, sometimes just to get though the day. Grief is messy and there was no roadmap my heart could follow. I had to feel my way through the darkness, while staying mindful not to make my home in the darkness.

It seemed easier to sit in dark corners than to walk forward with only enough light to see the step I was currently taking. I had to make friends with the unknown. Over and over again, I took the only step I could see—the one I was currently taking—and I had to consistently move myself out of the dark corners my heart frequently rested in.

Grief also taught me that my healing is tied to my willingness to adapt to change. What was for my highest good in year one would not be for my highest good now. What is for my highest good now would not have been healing for me in year two. And so it goes.

I am no grief expert and I haven't always served my own highest good. If I have done anything right in my messy world of mourning, it is simply that I have paid attention and course-corrected, over and over again. I have been mindful of what works, I have been mindful of what hasn't worked, and I have acted upon both.

When Perry died, grief became my new demanding family member who needed the biggest room in the house. Grief kicked me out of the driver's seat of my car and became my chauffeur. But these days, grief is more of a houseguest, or a backseat passenger.

Grief no longer needs to be a permanent member of my family, so I don't encourage it to be one. I allow myself to mourn, but I nurture my love. It's love that connects me with my son, and it is love that allows me to really see my people here, in body.

Some lessons I have learned from grief, and others I have learned from Spirit. My lessons in fear and shame, I have learned from both. Perry had been experimenting with a psychedelic drug when he died. He was not a drug user and our family had never faced addiction or substance issues.

Without warning, Perry died as a result of his decision to take a drug. I felt shame like I had never experienced about something we had never had to deal with. Then there was the shame I felt for being unable to save or even find my son.

I felt shame because of the collective shame we as a society have created around who we consider to be "good" or "bad" people, based on "good" or "bad" behaviors, even if I personally hadn't felt this way about other people. Shame gets passed down and spread around, and we become both sharers and recipients of shame. Until we release shame, fear, and judgment, we cannot fully see others as God sees them.

I have met so many children in spirit who have died from the disease of addiction. These young people were and are just as intelligent, loving, and loveable as my own children. These children were and are loved by their parents here, just as I love my children.

We will only be successful in helping individuals, families, and communities affected by addiction, and other social issues we face, when we turn the lights on shame. When we heal our own wounds, courage replaces shame and we begin to communicate authentically. Where we share our vulnerabilities, our weaknesses, our mistakes and our close calls, shame cannot survive. Where we communicate authentically, we create space for others to do the same, and we begin to see each other through God's eyes.

Through God's eyes we experience authentic connection, not just with Spirit but with each other, from a place of love and compassion. Through God's eyes, we see other people's issues, challenges, and struggles as God sees them. We see another's struggling spouse, sibling, friend, or child as our own.

Through God's lens of unconditional love and compassion, we can embrace ourselves in all our glory, and in all our struggles. When we offer ourselves unconditional love and compassion, this spills out onto others.

Perry taught me to see that our weaknesses are often flip-sides of our strengths or our strengths to the extreme. Yet we label "good" or "bad," which doesn't serve anyone. I admired Perry's brave spirit here, even though his immature bravery did give me cause for worry when he was here in body.

Perry was brave like I had never been in my life. Perry could also be reckless. I think of these two words, *brave* and *reckless*. I feel the very different connotations they inflict. Yet a person cannot be reckless without being brave.

It was a moment of recklessness that led to Perry's earthly demise, yet it was his bravery I loved most about him. I cannot separate one from the other and even if I could, I love the sum of his parts.

We do not need to be ashamed of who we are.

27

Lessons from Spirit

From Spirit, I have learned that spiritual seeking can be a tempting way to distract ourselves from grief, but we must not confuse spiritual seeking with spiritual connection. Spiritual connection may bring our loved ones to us, but it points us toward the view right in front of us.

Seeking keeps our heads in the clouds, but connection helps us learn how to live more fully here on earth, loving those beside us in body. It's why we are still here. Spirit wants to help us fulfill our soul's mission here. Our loved ones in heaven have already completed theirs.

I have learned that more healing is possible than we dare to imagine. We only limit ourselves. I've learned that each soul is here with a custom plan and individualized lessons to learn. My lessons may not be another's, but regardless of our path here, we all have within us the capacity to heal and grow.

Our loved ones on the other side live with purpose and sometimes this includes serving us, inspiring us, and teaching us here. I've learned that our loved ones are not all-knowing, but they do know our loving thoughts toward them.

Spirit has taught me that sometimes we don't receive

signs, not because we aren't paying attention, but because we aren't paying attention to us. My son started me out on this journey, and he has brought me full circle to know my own soul has all it ever needs—to heal, to connect with God, and to receive love. So does yours.

Perry, in spirit, has taught me lessons about the dynamics of our relationship now through visual metaphors and analogies. I previously mentioned I received signs from Perry when I began taking yoga classes. As time went on and I began to see the benefits of yoga for myself, the signs from him lessened. I had been pondering this just before arriving at yoga class one morning. During the class I saw a vision of Perry dropping weights down in front of me.

Perry encouraged me to get up and pick up the weights. This was demonstrative, for teaching purposes. He didn't want me to get up in that moment. I saw myself, through his perspective, picking up the weights. Then he brought the weights to me again, but this time he placed them farther away, yet closer to him.

This taught me two lessons. First, I must pick the weights up if I want to get stronger. The second lesson this taught me was that as I work at progressing in my healing, I move closer to where Perry lives.

Another interesting analogy Perry has shown me has to do with how Spirit sees us. One day Perry appeared to me in a vision as if he was outside, above our neighborhood. Maybe at the height of a hot air balloon or a low flying plane. From inside my house, I could only see what was within my house. I could step outside and see the neighboring houses, but my vision was still limited to the street we lived on. Perry looked down and saw our entire neighborhood spread out. This is how he sees our lives now. The neighborhood contains all the people he loves and has a soul connection with here. He sees us, all at once, from his new, broader perspective.

Perry showed me that he sees time in the same way. Past, present, and future is spread out like the houses in the neighborhood. Perry looked down the road to show me a house in the past, and up the road to show me a house in the future. At this point, I knew from my work and future validations that Spirit can indeed see around the corner and when it is for our highest good, Spirit can reveal this to us. I knew that time wasn't linear or sequential from Spirit's perspective. I really loved Perry's perspective and teaching demonstration about this. I can easily visualize the neighborhood and grasp, within my human reasoning, Perry's view of space and time.

The next analogy has to do with how we connect now. Perry showed me that he swims above the water, while he looks down and sees us as if in a submarine at the bottom of the ocean floor. He can dive down into the water to send me signs or make quick connections with me. He may dive down to drop signs so that I can see where they land from my submarine window.

Perry may look down and see that my mind is somewhat open (calm and still), so he dives down and yells a hello, creating a current that I can notice in my moment of stillness. I could be washing dishes when I hear his voice. He can share a memory this way as well. A memory of Perry or a fun time together comes to my mind, out of nowhere. I could be driving when this memory comes to mind. He may dive down and send me a hug this way. I catch the current, feeling his presence.

Maybe I experience a longer or stronger contact with Perry, such as these teaching visions I have received from him. In these moments, my energy is lighter, and I have risen above my submarine, where we meet closer to the middle. These are times when I may be fully present (undistracted) for an extended time, living in my higher self, above my lower or busy thoughts. For me, this is often in the morning, right after I wake up and before I begin taking in what is going on in the external world around me.

We must also consider that the highest good of all is always served. There are times we are quiet and at peace, yet that doesn't necessarily mean we will receive a sign from a loved one or discern their presence. This may circle back to the weight analogy, but there can be other reasons for this as well.

There is one big exception to the submarine connection analogy. I have been shown this exception not only from Perry, but from angels and other people's loved ones, while in connection with Spirit. In early grief, or when there is suffering here, heaven wants to step in. We, and our loved ones in spirit, have extra divine and angelic support during these times. With this extra support, heaven can meet us where we are to bring us healing, even if our submarine is at the bottom of Marianas Trench.

The shooting star we received at the perfect time didn't come directly from Perry, but all of heaven joined together and met us in our darkest hour, at our lowest point. Our star was God's way of letting us know our boy was safe, protected, and exactly where he was supposed to be.

My son's parting words spoken at the amusement park, "I'll always come home," have proven to be true. Every holiday, every birthday, and every anniversary, I have received signs from Perry. I have felt his presence. Not just on these days, but near these days as well.

When I hear Perry's voice, it is closer than my own

breath. This is not the relationship with my son I thought I would have, but I embrace the change. How blessed am I that my eyes have been opened and my heart expanded by my beautiful, blue-eyed wonder boy whom I loved, and love, more than life itself.

Epilogue

On our property in Tennessee, we raised hens. Eventually I even built up the courage to keep a rooster. We cooped our feathered girls at night and during the day they ranged on our land. One late morning, I heard a commotion and went outside to find the remains of three of our four red hens.

I picked Perry up from high school that afternoon and told him what happened while we were driving back home. As soon as I parked in our driveway, Perry jumped out and headed into the woods. I thought he might be trying to go find the predator.

About 30 minutes later my cell phone rang. I didn't get to my phone in time, but the call had been from Perry, which was odd because Perry was home, just outside. As I went to call him back, I noticed a text from him. Then a photo came through. It was a selfie of Perry with a broad grin on his face, holding a very alive hen that I had presumed was dead.

I laughed out loud in excitement, then Perry appeared in front of me. He had sent me the picture after coming into the house. He had been hiding just out of sight, waiting for me to see his text and wanting to witness my reaction. Perry had found our shell-shocked hen hiding in the woods. She had built up a nest of leaves around her, where she had most likely been hiding since the morning.

Perry taught me a lesson that day, and it is the same lesson he continues to teach me:

Now faith is the substance of things hoped for, the evidence of things not seen.

Hebrews 11:1

Acknowledgments

Thank you to Michelle Fairbanks, Melissa Williams Design, Julie Klein, and Kira Poncin for your professionalism and dedication to your craft and my story. I am most grateful for the way each of you put your talents and heart into this most personal endeavor for me. Thank you, Sally Walker, for helping me revise and keep my focus. Thank you, Jane Weaver, for your positive attitude and encouragement every step of the way. Cheers!

Thank you to all my family members who read what I know was not easy. Your blessing was my highest priority; thank you for approving of our stories that I shared. A special thank you to Sara Slagle, Rayanna Pearson, Jennifer Poncin, and Britta Pearson for your time and invaluable feedback.

Thank you to all my friends, clients, and supporters who so graciously approved of me sharing your story and/or your loved one's story. Thank you for cheering me on along the way. You have no idea how much your support motivated me to keep going when the weeks ran together.

I am grateful for all the loving people I have met since my forced plunge into the deep waters of my son's death. There are too many people to mention who have walked beside me. Thank you for giving me your literal or virtual shoulder to cry on. Simply knowing we walk together has given me comfort and infused me with strength.

Perry's friends and family, thank you for being the keeper and sharer of his stories. It means so much to me that Perry continues to be remembered on earth for who he was to you here. When my heart aches for his physical presence, it is soothed by knowing you will never forget our brilliant, adventurous, quirky, witty, one-of-a-kind, beautiful, blue-eyed boy for the amazing human he was.

Rayanna and Jonas, my love for you was God's grace on my darkest days. You are the very best brother and sister to Perry, and I know your shared memories are a gift he carries with him. Being your mother is a joy, and I delight in watching you become more of the unique and beautiful, true you.

Craig, your love and support for me and our children extends beyond the earth's limits. Thank you for being both my strongest and softest place to fall. I love you forever.

Perry, thank you for making me aware of this—

This book is my gift to you, your gift to me, and our gift to those it is meant to find.

Love you.

About the Author

Rachel is married with three children. She lives with her family; their dog, Finn; and cat, Ditto in Gilbert, Arizona. Rachel enjoys working from home, where she feels blessed to get up every day and connect others with their loved ones from heaven.

In addition to client sessions via phone and video, Rachel facilitates online discernment groups where she uses her intuitive abilities to help others discover and grow in theirs. Rachel offers occasional presentations and webinars to help others become more aware of the connection they already have, and will always have, with their loved ones in heaven. Rachel shares daily inspiration on her Facebook page Rachel Pearson, Spirit Messenger.

Rachel is a big fan of frequent, simple pleasures. Her favorite things are enjoying coffee in bed with her husband, spending time with her family, walking, yoga, and line dancing.

To learn more about Rachel or her services, please visit rachelpearson.net.

Made in the USA
Monee, IL
09 July 2023

38561069R00100